Adventurous Business
in
Costa Rica
or
Persistence Pays

Adventurous Business
in
Costa Rica
or
Persistence Pays

◆

A young salesman fighting corruption in
one of Central America's Banana
Republics (Story based on real events)

*"The perfect travel literature for sales people:
motivating, a page turner full of action."*

Ernst Muller

iUniverse, Inc.
New York Lincoln Shanghai

Adventurous Business in Costa Rica or Persistence Pays
A young salesman fighting corruption in one of Central America's Banana Republics (Story based on real events)

iUniverse books may be ordered through booksellers or by contacting:

iUniverse
2021 Pine Lake Road, Suite 100
Lincoln, NE 68512
www.iuniverse.com
1-800-Authors (1-800-288-4677)

ISBN-13: 978-0-595-40679-1 (pbk)
ISBN-13: 978-0-595-85043-3 (ebk)
ISBN-10: 0-595-40679-3 (pbk)
ISBN-10: 0-595-85043-X (ebk)

Printed in the United States of America

Contents

Introduction

-A Banana Republic

Close to Panama and Nicaragua there is a little country, where the organized crime from a German port city was able to establish a flourishing sex—and gambling business, and where one of the last presidents, used the publicity he gained by winning a Nobel peace price, to attract a locust like tourism business.

The little country, no more relying only on sex and gambling and promoting it's so called "eco tourism" has become a tourist magnet.

The proper citizens of that country, however, were only left with some poor paying jobs.
Not able to afford the expensive hotels set up for wealthy tourists, they are chased from their own beautiful beaches and other natural treasures.

Families like the one of the president's predecessors, who had accumulated their huge coastal properties often by questionable means, and a few rich and influential compatriots were the only beneficiaries of the wise policy of a Nobel price winner,—and of course the international tourism industry who perfectly knew how to take advantage of the corrupt and greedy Banana Republicans, willing to do everything for money, and who say of themselves: "We are country of Hijos de Putas" (sons of prostitutes)".

This into a tourist attraction converted Banana Republic has always been known as a sanctuary for the world's criminals and has a tradition for corruption.

In 2005, its last 4 presidents were indicted for taking bribes to award government contracts to foreign corporations.

One of these presidents, who are still at large, hiding in Switzerland, is the son of president Jepe (name changed) who plays an important roll in this book.

Another president, presently under house arrest, is the cousin of Caldera (name changed) who is the corrupt functionary in this book.

The entity, ITE (name changed), which awarded the questionable contracts in the case of all 4 presidents, is the same that published the tender which this book is about.

The only president who was not indicted, the Nobel price winner and pride of the country, changed the constitution to be reelected, after he failed to get his wife elected.

Law is bent whenever, wherever—if it is not for money then for power.

There are countless stories, books and films where the bad guys always take refuge in this adventurous country.
The reputation to be a sanctuary for criminals from all over the world, a heaven of the lawless and a playground for all kind of adventurers has been earned over many years. .
And there really have been and still are many criminals, even serial murderers who enjoy their live in this country close to Panama and Nicaragua.

There is hardly any place where child prostitution is tolerated as much as in that country. (Despite all the flyers at the airport, suggesting it is a crime.
But collecting money for the printing is one of these typical "chorizos" A slice of a "chorizo" (salami) is all it takes to do almost anything.

Retirees, most of them Americans, had a Permanent Residence Card for their entire life, until the law was simply changed and the Permanent Residence Cards were confiscated.

If one wants it his way:
-With money everything can be done
-just too bad to those who do not play by the rules of the game.

-Persistence pays

The story tells how international companies, playing by the rules of the game, influence the outcome of an international tender.

Bribery, violence and the involvement of internationally known politicians, nothing is sacred—if it helps to win the business.

And it shows how a young salesman, with determination and common sense, himself also employing very unusual methods, fights for his just cause.

The story is based on real events.

Some parts are seasoned with fiction.

Whenever deemed necessary, names of natural persons, corporations and the country where the events took place were replaced by fictive names. Ticos is how the Costa Ricans call themselves; Ticaragua stands for the Central American Banana Republic synonymous with Costa Rica

Names of internationally known politicians were left unchanged.

-The author

The author, who has lived in this Central American country for many years, released this story only after his departure.

Born at the German/French border, multi lingual, with a diploma in economics and business administration from the Frankfurt School of Economis, before setting up special "connection offices" for large international corporations in Colombia, Venezuela and Costa Rica to promote business with these governments was writing non fiction stories for newspapers about his adventures in the African Sahara dessert and the Sahel region.

His job, multi million dollar infrastructural projects requiring direct access to top government officials, made him expert in this highly corruptive business. Whether harbor cranes in South Africa, Angola and Mozambique, electrical Power stations in Egypt, Colombia, Costa Rica and Ecuador or special equipment for the police of some Banana Republic, he has many adventurous business stories to tell.

ICE ampliará la planta térmica de San Antonio

El Instituto Costarricense de Electricidad (ICE) compró dos unidades de turbina de gas, cuya capacidad de generación es de 20.000 kilowatts de potencia cada una, con un costo total de ¢ 38.179.000.

La compra se hizo a la casa fabricante en Alemania, AEG - KANIS - TURBINENFABRIK LTDA., mediante un préstamo que otorgó el Banco Mundial al ICE, en condiciones muy favorables. Se cubrirá con un plazo de amortización de 25 años, un período de gracia de cuatro años y medio, y un interés del siete y cuarto por ciento anual.

Según informó el gerente del ICE, Ing. Rodrigo Suárez Melido, las nuevas turbinas contribuirán a generar electricidad para satisfacer la demanda en las "horas pico", a partir de 1973.

En realidad se trata de una especie de ampliación de la planta térmica de San Antonio de Belén, donde también tendrán la función de trabajar como reserva.

El convenio que se firmó ayer en el edificio central del ICE, con participación de los señores Wiemth Middenhaue y Ernest Muller por la casa alemana, y del ingeniero Rodrigo Suárez Melido, licenciado Julio César Mora y los ingenieros Jorge Fajolo Quirós y Francisco Vargas por el ICE, — establece las siguientes obligaciones:

Las unidades deberán estar instaladas el 30 de diciembre de este año, una, la otra, 30 días después, o sea en enero de 1973.

En un aparte, funcionarios del ICE estimaron que las condiciones del empréstito, una indica que lo hace el Banco Mundial al país en poco tiempo, tan favorables para la institución, no significan otra cosa que "la confianza que tiene esta entidad bancaria en la capacidad técnica y administrativa del ICE".

Se dijo, además, que esta compra es la más importante, por su monto y justificación de inversión, que se hace en este año.

Agregaron nuestros informantes que también representa un paso más hacia el mejoramiento de los servicios eléctricos del país.

El ingeniero Suárez Melido, gerente del ICE, a la derecha, escucha atentamente la lectura del convenio, que hace el licenciado Julio César Mora. Lo mismo hace el señor Muller, a la izquierda, de la firma alemana. — (Aguilar)

PART I
Bribery

Chapter 1
The Hijacking

"You "hijos de putas" get up, move your asses, or this machete will teach you to follow my orders."

"Hey, you fat gringo," the hijacker shouted at Ernie's companion, "you sit there", he pointed at the last seat row, and looking at Ernie, he screamed "you take the seat next to him and shut up," he moved his long bush knife dangerously close to Ernie, "I told you to hold your mouth. You better believe me or I cut off your "cojones", it takes me one stroke."

There were caught in a brutal hijacking by Sandinistas, Nicaraguan rebels, who fought Anastasio Somoza, the notorious Central American Dictator, who ran Nicaragua like his own, private enterprise. Since the Somozas owned almost everything in Nicaragua, he held and treated his people the Nicas, how the Nicaraguans were called, worse than slaves.

◆   ◆   ◆

Ernie Piper EG's newly promoted sales manager had spotted a promising business: the turn key delivery of an electric power station with 4 gas turbines, each one with 20 megawatt, in Costa Rica, a Central American Republic. known for its bananas and coffee.

The project was called San Antonio according to the village where the plant was supposed to be built.
The financing came from the Worldbank.
EG was specialized in building such plants.
Ernie eager to prove that he was well able to handle his new job, contacted manufacturers for turbines and generators all over the world and finally brought a consortium together consisting of such reputable partners as:
EG/USA, Manis/Germany, Itachi/Japan and Tomble/USA

The leader of this consortium was EG, Schenectady. Ernie was in charge and it was his job to negotiate a contract with all partners, a so called consortium agreement.

The partners sent their engineers and calculators to already winterly Schenectady in upstate New York. It was only end of November. but a powerful snowstorm kept the visitors from around the globe inside the EG offices.

This was certainly a good omen. Even Mother Nature did its part to let the involuntary captives concentrate in elaborating a competitive bid.

The bad cold weather probably also did its part to agitate the imagination of a warm tropical country which was in reach for everyone if the bid was successful.

After more than 72 hours of continuous work, only interrupted by a few short naps, the aluminum boxes were closed and Ernie together with Otto Nunz an engineer from Manis the German turbine manufacturer were rushed to the regional airport in Albany.

Jordan Bryan an EG associate, known for his driving skills did the murderous trip through the blizzard, with his powerful BMW 720, endangering continuously the life of the three passengers and his almost new expensive car. There were stuck several times in high snow and had to shovel their way out.

Arriving at the airport in Albany only when the plane had already left its position, they were expedited in the ground manager's car to the Eastern Airlines 727 to Atlanta.

The boxes were loaded amidst the still blowing storm close to the runway. Due to this weather there were fortunately no incoming flights.

Otto and Ernie were upgraded into first class, or better, when boarding, they were told to take the next seat—and that was first class.

They were both totally exhausted.

The flight attendants probably felt sorry for them and wanted them to have a good time and a comfortable and relaxing flight.

When they were served dinner it was their first hot meal in more than 80 hours. They really enjoyed it and after a few glasses of wine they fell into such a deep and sound sleep, that the stewardess had problems to wake them up at their arrival in Atlanta.

It was after midnight, when they, after a 2 hours wait boarded a Delta flight to New Orleans. The blizzard had taken its toll on all flights.

They had missed the Eastern connection, were booked on Delta and got another upgrade into first class.

Finally after 2 am they arrived in New Orleans and looked for a quiet spot to continue their sleep.

At 7 am they boarded an old TACA, Lockheed Electra. TACA is the Salvadorian Air carrier.

Once inside the old propeller driven flying machine, they were in a different world.

The plane making frequent stops at all Central American airports on its way to Nicaragua was called "el lechero", the milkman.

The inside of the plane had already the ambience of the exotic world they were heading to. Seats, floors, walls—everything was covered with pink velvet.

Space was generous. The wide soft seats had a 2 x 2 pattern, always facing towards each other.

Immediately when the plane was airborne, the stewardesses, nice, friendly and sexy looking girls, offered liquor, though it was only little after 7 am.

When Otto and Ernie declined, they were compensated with even more seductive smiles and a delicious Salvadorian breakfast.

That was before their landing in Belize.

After Belize on their way to Guatemala, they gave in to the temptations and had a rum cocktail.

The sweet drinks and the even sweeter smiles of the two Salvadorian girls gave them a little anticipation of the world they were entering.

In Guatemala they had a delay of more than two hours due to some sort of rebellion in which four T33 fighter planes took part.

It was spectacular watching the planes dive and shoot. There were many explosions.

The airport was closed until the combatants returned from their mission. More rum cocktails were served during this wait. And the two friends lost in amorous conversations with their hostesses did not mind the extra time the plane was grounded in rebellious Guatemala.

When they finally arrived in Managua, their connecting flight with Lacsa, Costarrican Airlines, had already left more than 40 minutes ago. With lots of luck they were able to catch a Lanica, Nicaraguan Airlines flight to Panama from where they planned to take next morning, only hours before tender opening, a Costarrican Airlines flight to their actual destination, San Jose in Costa Rica.

The girls, the sweet cocktails, the Latin ambiente, everything had already taken its effect. They accepted this delay which was jeopardizing their entire work with an almost Latin attitude.

If they were not able to submit their bid the next morning punctually at 10 am they were out, all their efforts had been for nothing. These were the strict rules of public tenders.

◆   ◆   ◆

They had been airborne for approximately 20 minutes, when Ernie and Otto were torn out of their conversation.

Two men dressed in guayaberas, obviously Latin, in their mid twenties, were shouting and wildly gesticulating with pistols and machetes, long bush knifes.

"This plane is now under command of the FSLN. The new destination is La Havana in Cuba. If you follow our orders nothing will happen to you. Our fight is against Somoza, the murderer of our people, the ruthless dictator.

The cockpit door of the DC 9 opened and another man, also armed with a large pistol, became visible. There were at least three, perhaps even more, air pirates.

The Lanica DC 9 had five seats in a row, 3 on the left and 2 on the right side of the isle.

The hijackers started to reseat all 22 passengers, 20 men and 2 women. They wanted the front section of the plane cleared. The flight attendants, two women and one man, all in their twenties, had to take the very last row.

"Now it's our turn," said Ernie, "they are looking at us."

In contrast to Otto, Ernie had the "pinta latina" the Latin looks. He was of average height, dark hair, and dark eyes slim. Otto the engineer from Germany was a big man, 6 feet about 250 lbs, blond hair blue eyes with a big belly.

"Get over there, last row, the two seats on the right." bellowed the air pirate.
All orders of course were in Spanish. Good for Ernie and Otto that they spoke
Spanish almost as good as their native languages.

So when the pirate shouted his orders and vulgar threats, they understood everything.

"Las hembras also to the rear! Get your juicy asses moving, rapido, rapido."
The two women were sat in front of Otto and Ernie.

For the first time they met some resistance. The women were accompanied by
two men who did not accept being separated. They stood up, protested wildly
gesticulating and calling the pirates "hijos de puta".
All in a sudden one of the pirates who until now only had a watching eye on the
scene jumped forward and using the back of his machete he stroke one left one
right the two heroic protectors.
The strokes, though only given with the blunt side of the long bush knife, caused
some badly bleeding wounds on neck and head of the rebellious passengers.

One of the women, elegantly dressed with long black hair did not stop shouting
and insulting the pirates. Suddenly the same pirate who had already used his
machete caught her by the long hair and ritch-ratch off was her head's pride.
The woman was shocked. Her mouth stood open, all at once without hair, she
could not believe what had happened to her. She looked funny.
Nevertheless the situation was everything but funny.
"For heaven sake stay quiet now. No more heroes. This is not the place and time
for it." tried the male flight attendant to calm the heated tempers, "these people
are serious, and they make use of their arms. If one looses his nerves we all have to
pay for it. One single shot in this altitude will cause the plane to crash. So please
stay quiet and calm."

His appeal did not go unheard. It apparently had tranquilized groups, hijackers
and passengers. The pirates went to the front of the plane from where they were
able to control the situation. They gave their orders in a less aggressive way and
the passengers did quietly what they were told.
The pirates did not object dialogs between passengers as long as they were done
with a low voice. The passengers had to remain in their seats and were not
allowed to stand up.

"What do you make of all this? Do you think we spend the night in Cuba?" Otto thought it was time to exchange their views.

Ernie, whose parents immigrated from Germany, spoke fluent German. They did not want anybody to understand their conversation and therefore answered in his friend's language:

"Well I thought this only happens in the news or in movies. Now we are part of all this. I wonder what happens next."

Ernie liked adventures. This was something new; so far he was not worried. What could happen? These hijackers were no terrorists. They wanted to Cuba; they had no intention to kill anybody. As long as their demands were met, there was no imminent danger.

"The poor woman", Otto pointed at the funny looking head just in front of them. "This guy is very quick and accurate with his machete. I am sure he was serious when he threatened you, to cut off your "cojones". Good for you, you were able to control your tongue.

Otherwise your precious manhood would have been trashed together with this woman's beautiful long black hair.

Imagine all these beautiful senoritas in Costa Rica waiting for you. All you would have had for them: the story how you lost your "cojones".

"At least I would have had a story. I wonder what you will tell them.

I bet this machete artist works on a farm. These guys know how to perform such precise blows. So watch out, he called you a fat gringo. The way he said this, he dislikes gringos. He is watching you all the time, like taking measure for the surgical blow."

"I am glad you have not lost your sense of humor, Ernie. But look, we are not heading towards Cuba. Cuba is north-east—we are flying south-east. We are still heading towards Panama or even South America."

Otto was right. The sun was on their right side, almost behind them.

They looked out of the window. After a while the plane was loosing altitude and changing course to a north western direction. They were confused. They passed high mountains. They could clearly recognize a huge volcano. Then they saw a big city obviously in a high valley.

"A city surrounded by high mountains in this area that could be San Jose in Costa Rica."

Ten minutes later they landed in BR.

"Who knows, they probably ran out of fuel and are trying to refuel."

About 150 yards south west of the terminal the DC 9 came to a final stop. The engines kept running.

Nothing happened.
Time went by.
The hijackers were probably talking with the local authorities, negotiating.
Everybody was guessing. Only the "machete artist" was in the passenger cabin and watched every movement. After the demo with his machete he had everybody scared.
They all stayed in their seats and waited for something to happen.

Then two red fire engines moved quickly towards the plane. One stopped only twenty yards in front of the plane. The other one moved to the rear. They obviously tried to block the plane.

◆   ◆   ◆

The control tower at Coco airport in Costa Rica had been in contact with the hijacked plane previous to the landing. The authorities were informed about the pirates plan to fly the plane with all its passengers to Cuba. Refueling was urgently needed.
Air control immediately contacted the countries president, Don Jepe.
Don Jepe was an old revolutionary himself and had been a close friend of Fidel Castro who once regarded his friend Jepe as his mentor. When Fidel later went with the Soviets, and started to support Ticarauga's communist leader Manuel Mara s the friendship cooled down. Nevertheless Fidel and Jepe were still in good terms.
Don Jepe, now a social democrat had led the 1947 revolution and overthrown the corrupt government of president Caldera who was forced to take exile in Mexico. (These names and families play an important part later in this story.)

Don Jepe certainly happy to be torn out of his boring routine job as president of peaceful Costa Rica, was immediately taking charge of this hijacking affair. He saw the opportunity to demonstrate to his people, and the world that he had not lost his bite. He was still the fighter who ahead of all would lead his troops into combat.
He instructed Coco Airport to allow the Lanica plane to land and once on ground to block the runway with fire engines. Otherwise everything should wait till his arrival at the airport.

After his victory in 1947 Don Jepe had abolished the military in Costa Rica, making it the only state in America without military. The constitution allowed only a small police force, the so called Guardia Civil. This tiny force of several hundred men only equipped with light armory, had never been challenged.

Not wasting any time he commanded all available men to the airport with strict orders to wait for him, he would lead them to conquer the Nica—plane.

Once at El Coco, the airport, he stepped immediately in front of his men shouting;
"Adelante, vamos, we will show these Nica-caprones not to mess with our people."

That was the moment the fire engines, who previously had blocked the runway, went directly in front and behind the Nica plane and made it impossible for the plane to make any kind of maneuver .

The pirates aware that the plane was totally blocked and seeing armed men running towards the plane let the pilots feel all their fury and frustration. "You traitors have talked us into this refueling in Costa Rica. You pay for this."
And they took the pilot, led him to the cabin door, made him open the cabin door, pointed a pistol to his head, shot him and kicked him out of the plane.
From the moment the cabin door opened, this entire cruel scene could be watched by the storming president and his men.

They stormed forward and about 200 yards away they all started shooting at the plane as if the plane was to blame for the cruel murder.

Since the president and his men had all automatic weapons, machine pistols, nobody took aim. The bullets went everywhere.

Smoke started coming from the back of the plane, more smoke then flames. Something had caught fire. This looked bad.

◆   ◆   ◆

Otto and Ernie were well aware that the hijacking did not take its planned course. The situation was becoming more dangerous each moment. There were too many hot blooded and nervous people with deadly arms inside and outside the plane.
When Don Jepe with his Ticos attacked, many bullets made their way into the rear part of the DC 9. It was a miracle that nobody was hurt. But it was in the rear part where the smoke developed. The pirates were so engaged in the front section of the plane that they appeared to have lost interest in their hostages.

Being without vigilance crew and passengers openly discussed the situation. Their main concern was the smoke and the fire which any moment could spread and reach fuel.
The male flight attendant spread word around, that he was going to open the rear door and then everybody had to leave the plane as fast as possible.

When everybody had the message he quickly stood up and unnoticed by the pirates went to the very rear of the plane, released the door security and opened the door which automatically activated the stairway.

In less than 30 seconds the hostages had left the plane running towards the airport building.
They were still running when high flames came out of the plane.
Probably the open door letting air in caused the fire to develop rapidly.

◆   ◆   ◆

In the meantime Don Jepe and his men had shot their way to the airplane. Almost at the same time as the flames shot out of the rear of the DC 9 they took cover behind the fire engine which blocked the front of the plane.
They intensified their shooting now aiming at the front cabin door.

That was too much for the Nica hijackers; the rear of the plane in flames. The entire Ticaraguan police force only 20 yards away covered and protected by the fire engine, shooting like mad.

They made signs of surrender and when Don Pepe stopped the shooting, they came with raised arms to the front cabin door.

They were taken prisoners.

The captain who was believed dead was only slightly injured. He had been able to jump before the bullet hid his head. Unnoticed by anybody he took cover under the airplane.

Despite all the shooting there were no casualties. Some Ticos were injured; two of the hijackers were also injured.

Once the shooting stopped the firemen who had been on wait, rushed by and were able to extinguish the flames.

The DC 9 was badly damaged and remained close to the runway for a long time, witness of Don Jepe's glorious victory over the Nica air pirates.

The air pirates spent some time in a Ticaraguan prison and were then handed over to the Nicaraguan authorities. Somoza certainly made them pay for the loss of his new DC 9.

◆   ◆   ◆

The Nicaraguan hijackers did not make it to Cuba, but their intervention into Lanica's flight schedule benefited our two friends.

Instead of arriving in Costa Rica only the next day three hours prior to tender opening, they checked now into their hotel in downtown San Jose at 4 pm the day before.

Immigration and customs procedure was quick and friendly, more when the authorities became aware of their odyssey. The ride with an old Chevy along the 4 lane autopista framed with beautiful hibiscus hedges flowering coffee farms on both sides and 4 volcanoes clearly visible only a few miles away, was a first and very pleasant impression of this little known country. Traffic was light, the air felt good, the sun was shining and the temperature about 75 Fahrenheit.

What an exciting life. They were happy.

Downtown was different. The city was crowded, narrow, and dirty. The typical smell of tropical cities, sweet, foul, stinky; lots of beggars.
The streets full with people pulling or pushing hand carts loaded with almost everything one can imagine. The houses small, poor looking, tin roofs, all kind of colors. Many people barefoot, many drunken, stumbling around or simply laying in the streets.

Otherwise friendly faces, everybody seemed to have time, lots of beautiful girls, no fighting or visible aggression.

Their hotel, hotel Europa, said to be the best in town, medium sized, clean, very clean almost like a hospital in total contrast to the outside world. They got two nice rooms with view of the volcanoes and the busy Calle 1a, San Jose's Main Street.

They showered and changed clothes. Then they called their local representative. They never had done business with him before. The name was Ferreteria Croman.

Ernie called:"Mr. Frederico Croman please."
Answer: "Mr. Croman passed away two years ago."
Ernie looked in his booklet where all reps were listed.
There was also a Mr. Adolf Croman.
"Sorry to hear that Mr. Croman passed away. Let me talk to Mr. Adolf Croman."
Answer: "Mr. Adolf deceased 6 month ago."
What the hell was going on? Seemed to be an unhealthy climate.
"Listen, you are listed as our agent. We are from EG and taking part in ITE's public tender which opens tomorrow. We are at the Europa hotel."

"I am Mrs. Croman; I am now in charge of the business.
We are only minutes away from your hotel. We can meet in the lobby in half an hour. Then we can talk and see what we can do for you."

Precisely 30 minutes later two ladies entered the lobby and asked for Ernie. The elder lady was in her mid sixties, elegantly dressed, deep voice, probably a heavy smoker. The younger lady in her thirties was the daughter: blond, tall very German, arrogant.

After a formal introduction and a short chat, they were invited to the Croman residence. A chauffeur with a white Mercedes who had been waiting outside was driving.

They had a beautiful house with a tropical garden. Several servants offered drinks and appetizers.
They briefly discussed the tender and tomorrows bid opening. Mrs. Croman promised to send one of her staff, Jose, to accompany them to the opening.

Since the two friends did have a hard time behind them, they had not seen a bed for a week, they soon said good bye and went back to their hotel.
They both had a deep refreshing sleep. After a rich local breakfast, comprising of a sumptuous plate with all kinds of tropical fruits and the traditional "gallo pinto" black beans, rice, fried eggs and white cheese and several cups of cafe con leche, they were picked up by Mrs. Croman's chauffeur.

They went to the ferreteria, Mrs. Croman's business. The size of the company and the huge warehouses were impressing.

They were led into Mrs. Croman's office where they were offered more coffee.
After some small talk they came to business.
"Should we have a competitive bid, we need in order to become successful also some contacts within the ITE organization."
"Jose who will come with you to the opening is our salesperson for ITE. He has many friends and contacts within ITE."
"Mrs. Croman if you as our agent seriously want to help us to get this business, you have to have influential contacts within ITE." insisted Ernie.
"Well Mr. Piper, let's wait and see whether you are competitive, then we shall see further."

◆   ◆   ◆

And they were competitive.
Two hours later was the bid opening and everybody able to study their competitor's bids.

Everything was important. If the conditions of the tender specifications were not met exactly, the offer could be rejected. At least there would be a deduction of points in the later bid evaluation by ITE.

The competitors came from all around the globe.
There was Westinghouse and Pratt & Wittney from the US.
BBC from Switzerland, Siemens, Germany, JB from Scotland, Nuovo Pignone from Italy; Alsthom, France; Mitsubishi, Japan and last not least the consortium EG, Manis, Itachi, Tomble.
Most of the bidders knew each other from other similar projects.
The atmosphere in the canteen of the old ITE facilities at the Parque Moran was tense.

When the head of ITE's law office Lic. Tulio Nota with a solemn voice started reading the prices, it was quiet like in a tomb. Everybody was taking notes.

The consortium's price was the last one read.
Ernie and Otto stopped breathing, they had the lowest price and the best offer.
They were followed with notable differences by Westinghouse and JB.

Ernie was the one who had this unconventional idea to form a partnership of suppliers, a consortium. So everybody was responsible for his own part. No unnecessary risk factors, no double overhead charges—a streamlined concept which would guarantee minimum prices.

Everybody was talking about the EG consortium. They met looks with respect and looks with envy. Many especially the ones who could not compete, their prices being absurdly high, came and shook hands with Otto and Ernie, congratulating them.
Of course this business was far from being won, but it was a very promising beginning. They had won a decisive battle. They felt proud.
They, both newcomers, novices were challenging all these famous companies from around the world.
Now they had to make sure that the next steps were right. Some competitors would just walk away; others would do what ever it takes to improve their position. That was normal.
The economic situation worldwide was not good. There were not to many of these projects and a 50 million $ business nobody could afford to miss.

This was now entirely Ernie's job. Otto was mechanical engineer, specialized in gas turbines. If technical details had to be worked on, Otto would take care of that or get help from the other partners.

At least for the next 90 days, the time set for the evaluation, the fight was on. Once the evaluation completed, the best bidder would be allocated and a contract would be negotiated and signed.

The critical period was between now and the allocation. All bidders who after this opening decided to stay in the race would fight.

The consortium's favorable position had to be defended. Ernie desperately needed somebody inside the customer's organization to keep him posted about every new development. He had to be able to react immediately.

He soon would find out who their toughest competitors were.

Key question was now: Were there any commitments between ITE's decision makers and competitors. Had money been exchanged or promised to do certain favors e. g. for a more favorable evaluation or even the allocation of the business. They probably would soon know one way or the other.

Otto and Ernie closed their briefcases and left the battleground with a victorious smile on their faces.

Chapter 2
The Bribing

Two month prior to these events an elegantly dressed man, probably in his early forties, arrived at El Coco airport in Costa Rica.

A local observer would have judged him to be a wealthy Italian or Argentine businessman, not only because of his expensive outfit but also the self assured and just appropriate way he moved and talked to the airport authorities was typical for the image Ticaraguans, or the Ticos how they called themselves, had of their latin brethren.
In front of the terminal he was welcomed by a man dressed in the traditional white Guayabera, the button down shirt which like a jacket was worn over the pants. He measured more than six feet and was bald, although he could not be much older than thirty years.

"Bienvenido a Costa Rica, Juliano," and pointing at a small Hartman leather case he asked, "Is this your only luggage?"
"I usually travel only with carry on luggage, makes me faster and more flexible.
Good to see you Fernando.
My wife always jokes saying I had more homes than suit cases.
Well everybody has a little spleen."

"Let's go to my car, Juliano. I do not want somebody sees us together."

Fernando Caldera, chief engineer of the engineering department of the "Instituto Ticaraguense de Electricidad", the state owned Ticaraguan utility company, short ITE, climbed into a green Land Rover opening the passenger door from the inside.

"We will drive to a small coffee finca (coffee farm) only ten minutes from here. It belongs to an associate of mine, nobody will disturb us there."

"Fine with me Fernando, I am coming from Caracas where I have a project similar to the one here.

It would suit me much, if we could come to terms, so I can take the PanAm evening flight. In that case I am able to meet with my family tomorrow in New York."

"Well Mr. Maldecara," Caldera was becoming formal, "that is up to you. I look forward to your proposition."

In the meantime they had arrived at the coffee farm. A man dressed the same way as Caldera about his age, welcomed them in front of a large "casona" the typical Ticaraguan farmhouse, traditionally built from clay. Caldera introduced his associate as senor Nieto.

"Mr. Nieto is my associate in a construction and engineering company which we both own. This company has experience in doing civil and mechanical work for projects like the San Antonio gas turbine plant."

Malcecara understood the hint—could not have been any clearer.

They walked into the cool farmhouse. Typical for these houses it had huge terraces all around the house. There were many benches, rocking chairs and hammocks all located in pleasant shady places. The inside was furnished with dark heavy mahogany furniture in Spanish colonial style.

They took their seats around a coffee table.

"Feel in your own house Don Juliano", that was the traditional Ticaraguan welcome. "What can I offer you? Did you have lunch on the plane?" Mr. Nieto was a polite host.

"Oh yes, there was plenty of food. But I would appreciate one of your famous coffees."

Nieto called for somebody. Immediately a girl dressed in maids uniform entered. He ordered coffee for three and some cookies.

Waiting for the maid to return, they exchanged the usual courtesies and had some small talk. The coffee, consisting of one third "tinta" extremely strong black coffee, and two parts of milk, was served.

Now they started talking business.

"Senores, no bad feelings, but I would rather have this conversation just between the two of us, Fernando and I. Mr. Nieto this is no mistrust, just a matter of principle."
Nieto rose without comment and left Caldera and Maldecara alone.

Maldecara started;" I have received the preliminary tender specifications four weeks ago. My client is willing to participate and believes he can prepare a competitive bid. I have with me his suggestions, where and how he wants the specifications changed. That would give him certain advantages towards his competitors."

Caldera was listening, Maldecara sipped from the delicious coffee.

"Despite these advantages," continued Maldecara, "there are limits as far as up markings for kick backs or commissions are concerned. Including a full 10% as suggested at our last meeting, my client fears, his price will become too high. And defending a price which is exaggeratedly high will be very difficult since the entire project is financed by the World Bank.
They usually do not interfere, but their approval is still needed.
He is suggesting to leave it at 3%, which would bring it to 1, 5 million $ for you and your friends.
This also would make your job much easier. The less difference in price exists the less you have to worry about appeals."

"Juliano as you well know this money has to be shared with other people. I first have to discuss this proposal with them before I can make any comments. If you would please excuse me, I have to make a few phone calls."
Caldera rose and went somewhere in the house to get hold of his friends. Whether he really talked to somebody or he was only acting … who knows.

After 10 minutes he returned. "Juliano if your people can not be competitive including 5% for us, we are not interested. This is our last word. However, before we make any further commitment you have to release his name."

"Let me talk to them first, Fernando, to see whether this is agreeable.
Then you get their name.
Can I can make an overseas phone call?'

"Well, Juliano we are in Costa Rica, not in the United States. We can try. I get the international operator for you."

Maldecara was lucky, within moments he had his party on the other side of the Atlantic. And without any major discussion he even got his party to agree to the Caldera's proposal.

Caldera returned immediately when Maldecara hang up.

"Fernando we have a deal. Your proposal was accepted by: you know the guys "JB", the UK manufacturing associate from GE.

You get 1% with allocation, 3% when JB gets his payment from the Worldbank and the final 1% against letter acceptance, well probably your own letter."

They shook hands and the business was firmly committed to JB.

It would be almost impossible for any other bidder to beat this alliance.
Caldera as the engineer in charge could influence conditions and specifications so they were tailor made for JB. Later he would be in charge of the evaluation team and it was his job to make the recommendation for the allocation by the board of directors. Caldera had committed part of the kick back money to others who had themselves committed to support him.

In Andy Quarry, ITE's president, JB had another unexpected supporter. Andy May proud of his Scottish heritage would do everything to give support to JB who forms part of the famous Scottish shipbuilder.
As one of the president's veterans from the 1947 revolution, Don Andy enjoyed every support from Costa Rica's president.

Juliano Maldecara himself was a legend. There was nobody in the gas turbine business who had not heard the fancy stories about Juliano.
He had arranged similar projects in all countries where gas turbine power-or pipeline compressor stations were needed.
His wealth and cosmopolitan lifestyle was society gossip as were his luxurious residences in Rio de Janeiro, Estoril and Manhattan.
His world wide network of mostly personal connections and his intelligent sales strategies had made him the most successful agent in the gas turbine business.

◆   ◆   ◆

When Mrs. Croman, the consortium's representative learned the news about the consortium ranking first among all bidders, this was as good as if the business was already in her pocket.

After a sumptuous lunch to celebrate the event, she suggested;" Allocation is set for mid February. Nothing will happen before January 15th. This time of the year everybody is busy with Christmas and New Year. Many travel to Panama or Miami for shopping.

You both did an excellent job, return home to your families enjoy the holidays. We take care of everything here."

"I am spending the weekend at our beach house in Guanacaste with my boy-friend." it was the first time the Croman daughter said something.

"Come with us, I am sure you will enjoy it."

Otto who had in fact finished his job agreed to accompany them.

Not so Ernie.

He was determined to establish a contact to one of the engineers of the evaluation team.

He suggested to Otto before leaving for the beach to pay ITE an official visit and to introduce themselves as the first ranking bidder.

They had a great advantage before the other bidders. He was going not only to defend this advantage but to build on it till they really had the business in their pocket.

He would try to convince his boss, to let him stay and personally take care of things.

The company's rep was for no use. Had they known before, most likely they had not taken up this project. That was his mistake. He should have contacted the agency before even touching this project.

Normally one only gets involved in a rather complicated government business like this after making sure that there is a reliable agent with the proper connec-tions.

They could not leave this business to the absolutely unprepared and disinterested ladies. That would be the end of this so promising business.

He met Otto in the lobby of their hotel. "Otto can we make this trip to the volcanoes instead of tomorrow morning in the afternoon.
Being the first ranking bidder, we need to introduce ourselves to the ITE engineers. Let's do this tomorrow in the morning. After that we have some leisure time." Otto agreed.
"I am going to call my boss now to give him the good news and see what he has to say. We can meet at the bar in about an hour, if you like, to have our own celebration."

Ernie called his boss HH, short for Henry Higgins in Schenectady.

"HH, I have good and bad news—which one first?"

"I had a bad day, give me the good news first."

"We have the best bid with the lowest price, we are ranking first."

"That is probably because the non US-bidders are all including kick back money to get the business.
Anyhow very good news—thanks to you putting this consortium together and excluding unnecessary overheads.

What's the bad news?"

"There is no real agent. We have to do everything ourselves. The agent listed in our records has passed away—the successors: two weird ladies."

"Blame yourself Ernie; you should have gotten some information about the agent's situation before even taking up the business.
How do you want to handle it now?"

"I am trying to establish a contact within the client's engineering team and work directly with him."

"That won't be easy; these businesses especially in that part of the world are mostly sold before the tender is even published. Let me know when you have your contact. When is your trip back?"

"Next week, I'll be home for the holidays."

"Okay, good luck, have a safe trip."

Ernie hung up. This conversation did not go the way he intended.
HH had an answer for everything and the blame concerning the agent was right to the point. Well therefore he was the boss.
Ernie was young and without experience, he would learn.
It would have been counterproductive if he had asked now for a permission to stay in Costa Rica in order to take care of everything himself.
He would do that personally, when he was in the office in Schenectady.

Otto and Ernie met at the hotel bar, had a few drinks and some "bocas", appetizers.
Both were single and were anxious to learn more about the "Ticas", the Ticaraguan girls with a reputation of being beautiful and sexy.

The cabdriver knew exactly what they were looking for. He drove them to George's, a cozy little bar, packed with young, beautiful and really sexy girls. The atmosphere was peaceful, clean and non commercial.

They ordered drinks and invited the most appealing girls to join them.
It did not take long and Otto was totally lost. He only had eyes for a black haired, black eyed, perhaps 18 year old girl, with very sensual lips. She knew how to handle men like Otto.
She teasingly played with her tongue pretending to moisten her lips, looking deep into Otto's eyes. Moving closer to Otto she put her hand on his thighs and soon letting him explore her sensual mouth himself.

Ernie enjoyed sitting between two girls who gave him a similar treatment with twice as much fun. He enjoyed the relaxed environment, which at the same time was loaded with erotic and the simple joy of living.
This was different to anything he had ever seen in the States. Everybody had fun.
At some point money probably discretely changed its owner. But one was not even sure about that.
There were only a few men in the bar.

Ernie was talking to the bartender. Her name was Olga. On their way to the bar, the cabdriver had already told her story. Olga was the only daughter of Manuel Mara, the leader of Costa Rica's communist party and close friend of Fidel Castro.

"You are wondering why I am here," she said in perfect English so nobody was able to understand her, "I was so crazy to associate myself with an American. His name was George. A few months ago I caught him with one of the girls. Well that was the end. Costa Rica is a man's land.
But I had a different education, I have my own rules," and she added laughingly, "I am my father's daughter."

"George left me this place. I want to sell it. But times are bad. What are you doing here? Why don't you buy it," she said teasing him.

"You can handle a couple of girls at a time; you are the right man for this business."

When she was talking to Ernie, the two girls were giggling and fumbling him. They had fun; so had Ernie.
One had long blond hair, blue eyes and an almost white skin. The other one was Chinese. Beautifully shaped almond eyes, perfect skin and body. They coordinated their efforts and softly pressed against Ernie's vulnerable parts. Ernie could not wait any longer.

Around 3 am he called Otto in his room.
"Just checking, are you still alive. I did not know you enjoy this kind of pleasures too."

For a few hours they had forgotten their job. The next morning they met for breakfast and discussed the planned visit to ITE.

"Otto more as a pretext, I would like you to explain to the ITE engineers the advantages of the GE turbines over Pratt & Wittney's jet engines, the Westinghouse systems and the little experience Siemens and BBC have. For technical questions they only accept an engineer they would not take me serious."

They stopped a taxi in front of the hotel and went to the ITE offices. There they asked to meet with the engineers from the engineering department.

They did not wait long, when a European looking gentleman greeted them at the same time rapidly speaking German, English and Spanish.

"Guten Morgen, good morning, buenos Dias," it is a great pleasure, eine grosse Freude, to welcome you. I am Jorge Lappa, mechanical engineer.

Please follow me to my office."

He had a little office which he shared with his colleague Antonio Cargas.

"Gentlemen I am glad you came. I had a brief look at your bid. It appears that you strictly adhered to all tender specifications. And your price is the lowest of all bidders. Of course we have to make our evaluation, there will be points given and taken."

"Certainly" answered Ernie, adding, "The purpose of this visit is to introduce ourselves. It is always good to know each other personally.

If there are any questions we would be delighted to answer them."

"This is a wonderful idea; I also like to know the people I am dealing with." And looking at Otto he continued, "I understand you are German. I am from Hungary. I like Germany and Austria. My oldest son was born in Vienna. In 1956 we were fleeing from Hungary. I hate the Sowjets, they shot at us. My first wife could not bear all this; she died in Austria shortly after giving birth to our son."

The door opened, a tall bald man entered, he could not be older than 30 years, dressed in a white Guayabera.

"May I introduce the gentlemen," Lap had hastily stopped his private story, "this is Mr. Ernest Piper from EG and Herr Otto Nunz from Manis in Deutschland." and turning around "this is Ingeniero Fernando Caldera, my boss and head of the evaluation team.

They briefly shook hands said a few words and Lappa's boss was gone. Lappa had changed. He seemed to be afraid of his boss. He was glad when Otto and Ernie left his office.

"Where are you staying," asked Lappa in German.

"At the hotel Europa," answered Otto.

"I call you in 30 minutes"; promised Lappa, "wait for my call."

They shook hands.

◆   ◆   ◆

"That was a short good bye after all this familiarities," wondered Otto when they tried to stop a taxi.

"Wait, there is more to come. I would not be surprised if this man becomes our so desperately needed contact."

Once at the hotel they went immediately to Ernie's room waiting for Lappa's call. Exactly half an hour after they had departed from the ITE offices the telephone rang and Lap was on the line.
"I would like to invite you for a drink and some bocas at my home. It is so seldom, that I meet people with who I can chat about the old world."
Ernie could not refrain asking a little cynically: "So Otto comes alone?"
"Why are you asking this?"
"Well, I am from the new world and don't know much about Austria or Germany."
"Oh there are other more important things you and I have to talk about."

Lappa asked them to take a taxi and be at his home by seven pm. He gave exact directions.

Now Ernie and Otto had something to discuss.
"I bet he wants to work with us. Now we have to know under what conditions. Since you have plans for tonight Otto, I can handle this by myself. He doesn't really want to talk about Europe anyhow.
This Lappa is not the one who makes decisions but he could be a valuable informant and that is what we need most, at least for now."

Otto agreed. That was not his job anymore. Sales and respective arrangements, that was up to Ernie. His mind was set to have some more fun. Who knew, whether he ever came back to this little paradise?

The phone rang again. This time it was Mrs. Croman's driver to pick them up for the volcano sightseeing tour.

They had an interesting time seeing the beautiful countryside and walking around the crater of the Yrazu volcano. It was still very active and only had erupted a few years ago, covering part of the "meseta central" the high valley with ashes.

Back at the hotel they still had to make their flight arrangements for their return home, something they had entirely forgotten.

They showered, to get rid of the fine grey volcano dust and then every one took off to his date.

◆　　◆　　◆

6.30 pm, it had been night for an hour, it was raining. Very few street light, dark—Ernie in a taxi was heading to Lap's home. They passed a long narrow one lane bridge. "El puente los Anonos", built by the American corps of engineers, explained the cab driver, "it spans a small river which with these torrential rains has become a dangerous stream." Then he added," It's the favorite spot for people to commit suicide."
Ernie was shivering: the darkness, the rain, the bridge, the story really creepy and scary.
A little later they arrived at Lappa's home.

A high iron fence protected the house. Lappa was waiting in front of the house. Ernie paid the cab and went inside. Lappa introduced him to his much younger wife and his 14 year old son from his first marriage.
They had a drink and some bocas together with his wife and son before going into a nice little library.
Once undisturbed and by themselves Lappa came quickly to the point.

"You are both leaving Costa Rica within the next days but you are not too happy leaving this promising business in the hands of your agent.

This used to be a very good agency. When the old man Don Frederico died, things changed. His son in law, Don Adolfo who was in charge only a short time before he also passed away, was "un inutil, un pendejo" as is his daughter. You know what I mean,—not worth a dime.

Once you are out of the country, your competitors will do anything, to take your place in the ranking. With the backing, some of them have this will happen soon. I know for instance that Caldera has been talking several times with somebody he called Juliano. I am not sure who Juliano is working for.
I myself was approached twice for support against payment. But I am still uncommitted."

"So what do you suggest, Mr. Lappa?"

""I would be interested to permanently improve my monthly income.
I know that your agent is looking for both a technical and a financial advisor.
I would be interested in the technical job. It would be a permanent job which I could do perfectly besides the job I have with ITE. And it would be legal."

"Well Mr. Lappa let me discuss your proposal with our agent. I promise to let you know what we can do, before I leave Costa Rica."
"

Lappa offered to drive Ernie to the hotel. "It is difficult to find a cab to pick you up here. We are a little far out here and then this heavy rain. They are afraid of getting lost."

Lappa had a little Datsun. They took the same way as Ernie did on his way out by taxi.
The weather had become worse.
Total darkness except for the car's headlights and the parking lights of a car behind them. Strange, why would somebody drive in that darkness and rain with nothing but parking lights.
Well perhaps some electrical defect and the driver taking advantage of Lappa's car leading the way.

The car, it seemed to be a big car, had been behind them since they passed the big mango tree, a landmark, some 200 yards from Lappa's house.

The car closed up, it was now directly behind them; bumper to bumper. Lappa was getting nervous.
Then suddenly getting on the "suicide bridge" with only one lane, all lights went on, the car pulled next to them, hit the car's side where Ernie's was sitting, a pow-

erful flashlight was aimed at Ernie's face, blending him and Lap and passed accelerating very fast.

Lappa lost control of his car and could not avoid hitting the bridge's iron railing on his side of the car.

Although they could not make out the license plates, everything went so quickly, they still were able to see that it was a huge dark car, Cadillac or similar. A car they would easily recognize. There were not many big black American cars in Costa Rica—and from hitting Lappa's car it had a scratch on its left side.

"That was close." was all they could say

Lappa stopped directly behind the bridge to assess the damage. Lappa could live with it since the little Datsun had already had lots of scratches before.

Ernie looking down from the bridge some 200 feet below he could more hear than see the waters of what was now an uncontrolled stream. He shivered: "Well not a good place to end one's life."

On their way to Ernie's hotel Lappa said: "We have to be careful. We should not be seen together in public anymore. Somebody was desperate to see who was with me.

Well, now they know, there is nothing we can do about that. It was nobody from ICE, that's for sure."

Once in his hotel room, Ernie immediately called the agent, Mrs. Croman.

It was late, but so what. The agent would get a commission of one million $ probably even more. She should do something for that money.

The consortium needed Lappa, he was better than relying exclusively on the agency.

He had a heated discussion with Mrs. Croman.

Mrs Croman acknowledged that she was looking for a technical advisor. So why not Lappa?

This was the biggest business the agent ever had.

So why not take this opportunity and fill this vacancy with somebody the consortium desperately needed.

At some point Ernie told her

"If you do not cooperate with us, we see another agent. For a commission of more than one million $ we will get all the help we need. Think about it—if I do not hear from you by tomorrow, I will get a decision from the consortium."

Ernie was in no mood to leave the hotel. He went to the hotel bar and had a couple of drinks and then went to bed.

Early next morning the Croman daughter and her boyfriend came to pick Otto up for their trip to the beach. She said her mother wanted to talk to Ernie, and meet with him at the agencies office as soon as possible.

Ernie had breakfast and then went to the agency.
Mrs. Croman had changed completely, whether it was Ernie's announcement to take the agency away from her or that she reflected what her father would have done in this situation. She seemed to be willing to cooperate.

"Mr. Piper I thought about our discussion and I agree we need somebody for this business who is more qualified than the salespeople we have now selling cable and electrical material to ITE.
I personally do not like Mr. Lappa. He is not sincere and talks too much."

Ernie had to agree, her judgment about Lappa was about right.

"We contracted a financial advisor. He is an accountant, CPA and oversees our bookkeeping and advises us in financial matters.
He is a good fried of Lic. Nota, ITE's lawyer, you met him at the tender opening. He is the one who read the bid prices.
His name is Hernan Fonseca and he will be here any minute.
Feel free to talk to him and ask him whatever is on your mind. He is discrete and trustworthy."

Hernan Fonseca entered the office. He was a very big man almost as high as wide. He was about thirty, had great problems with breathing but otherwise an intelligent and sharp man. He talked only when necessary, listened and immediately understood Ernie's worries.
Ernie had to admit, Fonseca had a winning and pleasant personality. He was a person one would associate with and trust much easier than Lappa.

"So you are friend of Nota, the ICE lawyer?" Ernie asked him after they had talked a little about the economic situation in Costa Rica.

"Yes Tulio and I have been friends since we were kids."

"Why don't you call him right now and tell him that you and we intend to work together and what your odds are if you do that on a commission basis?"

A moment later Hernando was talking to his buddy Tulio.
They could hear him ask the question and see Hernan listening a while.
Then Fonseca asked Lic. Nota:
"Tulio you probably already reviewed the legal and commercial part of their bid. So far any comments?"

Hernan listened and shortly thereafter the conversation was ended.

"Julio thinks it is a great idea you and me working together. He confirmed that you are ranking first and that he could keep a watchful eye that it remained that way. He is going to discuss details personally with me; not on the phone.
He had already reviewed your legal and commercial part and did not find anything that would jeopardize your ranking."

They left it at that and Ernie went to Mrs. Croman's office to give her his decision.
He was not sure. This Fonseca was a nice bright guy and seemingly was well related to Nota. To have his advise and Nota's support could not hurt and could become important at a later stage.

"Fonseca could become a valuable asset;
Not only his friendship with Nota but more even his advice and cooperation.
But, neither Nota nor Fonseca have access to the information we need from the engineering department.
Although I share your feelings about Lappa, he is the only one who can help us there. Why don't you give him the job he wants and tell him that you are only going to keep him, if he proves to be helpful to get us this business."

Mrs. Croman accepted Ernie's proposition.

◆   ◆   ◆

The same day the tender was opened and the bid prices publicly read Caldera was called by his friend Juliano Maldecara.

"How did the bid opening go, where are we?"

"You are ranking 3rd, about 200,000 $ higher than Westinghouse and 800,000 $ higher than the EG consortium."

"That is HH. He used to be VP sales for gas turbines with GE." Juliano sounded a little worried. "So what do you think?"

"To be frank, I was a little disappointed. After reducing our money so drastically, I thought you would come in much better. You are far apart from EG."

"They did this as a consortium, which is always cheaper. We had no idea somebody would do that. It's not easy to get these guys under one hat. They usually compete against each other"

"Well EG did it. It makes things very difficult for me."

Caldera obviously wanted to increase his money. Maldecara got the message but he did not comment on it. He knew HH; he would fight, especially when he knew that Juliano Maldecara was behind it. He had kicked HH out of a big project in Argentine which HH almost had pocketed.

"Fernando, I hope your people are still firm behind it?"

"You know how these things are, if they can get more and if it is easier—who knows, you never can be sure."

"I saw this coming it's always the same. The slightest problem and the rats desert ship, they think it's sinking.
I hope that's not the case. You still get lots of money. And you get it, to solve these kinds of problems. You know that, you have done this before. Who is it you

are not sure of? We have to know who he is siding with. I have people in Costa Rica who can handle this."

His conversation with Caldera finished, Maldecara made another call to Costa Rica.
"David it's me, I need you to do me a favor." And he explained to David Levy a former CIA and Mossad agent that there was a potential that somebody from the engineering or legal department at ITE might look to associate with some of the bidders.
"Just keep me informed, so far no other action is needed."

This done, he made another call, this time to JB in Scotland.
He needed to discuss with Mr. Duncan, VP Sales of JB the results of the Bid opening.
"Mr. Duncan you know, you only made third place despite tailoring this tender exactly as you wanted it, to give you an advantage over the other bidders. Our friends at ITE are somewhat disappointed. They say it will be hard to overcome a difference of 800,000 $ towards the top ranking bid.
I only wanted to make sure you knew, just in case, if more incentives or technical assistance from one of your engineers is needed."

So that done, he went to his associate Ernst Sommer next door. Ernst was his lawyer, adviser, confidant, partner and friend.

"We have a problem in Costa Rica. After bid opening we are only third, although everything was tailor made for JB. To enter with a low price EG has formed a consortium with Manis and Tomble,—very clever.

Everybody is backing us, so normally we would not have a problem.
But the price difference is substantial and the business is financed by the World-bank. They usually do not interfere but they still have to approve the allocation.
And EG means that HH is behind it. If he becomes aware that I am in, he will fight. He takes this personal.
Can you find out who exactly is handling this business in Costa Rica?
I heard from my ITE contacts that they have no real agent and the one who presented the bid, the project manager, is a young guy whose name is Ernie Piper."

Two days later Maldecara called David Levy.

"What did you find out Dave?"

EG is very active. Their guy, Ernie Piper visited Lappa at his home and stayed there for almost two hours. I identified him on his way back to the city. Lappa is a nervous man. I had to pass him to verify who he was with. He got so scared that he lost control of his vehicle and almost made a dive from a bridge."

"But David was it necessary to identify his company in such a spectacular way?— They know now that they are being watched and will be very careful."

"Or Lappa ceases to support them, because he is now too scared." answered David, "but this Piper is very active. It is difficult to catch up with him. He met yesterday morning with "El Gordo" Fonseca consultant and adviser of many large corporations in Costa Rica and an intimate friend of Lic. Nota, ITE's lawyer. Nota seems to be with them at least for the moment.
Piper leaves tomorrow for the US but made reservations to be back by January 15th."

Maldecara was satisfied with David's job.
What concerned him was how vigorously this young Piper was trying to get support from inside the client's organization. He clearly had already identified where his weaknesses were. Not bad for a young inexperienced guy. He should not be underestimated. Naivety can generate unknown energies and generally makes one do things in a way that is different and incalculable for the opponent. Yes naivety could well be an asset.
He felt himself reminded of his early days in this business.

◆   ◆   ◆

Ernie had indeed made his reservations for Saturday. Before leaving he needed to talk to Lap. Lap was still scared of what had happened the evening they met.
Finally they agreed to meet in "La Cascada" a restaurant which was close to his home.

"Mr. Lappa, I talked to our agent and she agreed to give you the job you suggested. But she will only keep you if you show that you can and do support our cause.

We do not need to improve our ranking,—we are first. All we expect from you is to keep us informed if somebody else is trying to influence the evaluation and to take our place or if somebody within your team is manipulating things to change the ranking of the competitors.

You know how to reach me, please call me immediately if there is a reason to be concerned."

They left the restaurant. In a booth behind them somebody had heard every word of their conversation.

◆   ◆   ◆

Ernie had two more days in Costa Rica. He had booked for Sunday. Otto was supposed to be back the same day from the beach. There still would be enough time to meet.

After his meeting with Lappa he went downtown to do some Christmas shopping.

That done he really had nothing more to do for the next two days.

He went to Georges. It was still early. Olga was there and two girls.

"Ola Ernesto, I hope things worked out for you the other night."

"One could not have asked for more."

"So you are back for the next two."

"No I was feeling like some good company, you are the reason I am here."
"Don't get the wrong idea, I am not available."
And the way she looked at him made it even clearer. Olga was a lady, she had class. The way she moved, dressed and talked. She was the daughter of one of the most reputable politicians.
She was a beauty.
Two years ago she won a beauty contest and became Miss Costa Rica.
Dark eyes, sensual lips, perfect white teeth, immaculate white skin, long legs, beautiful body, and long black hair—everything a man could dream of.
"Well Olga, we will see I am going to test your honesty."

Ernie spent all the evening at the bar, joking with the girls, but he did not hide that his main interest was Olga.

When he later asked Olga whether she would show him her favorite beach, she knowing that he had only two days left, agreed to pick him up next morning and take him to Puntarenas a port town with beach at the Pacific Ocean.

At 6 am Olga was at the hotel. She was driving an old Land Rover.
After driving along coffee farms and sugar plantations they arrived three hours later in Puntarenas.
They changed to their bathing outfit inside the car and then immediately dived into the warm water of the Pacific.
Olga was just breathtaking.
Never had Ernie felt so attracted. The warm water, the black sanded beach, the tropical heat, her sensual body, her skin smoothly touching his—only the fishermen watching them, held them back to let nature take its course.
They had a wonderful time: swimming, diving, touching, and kissing.
For lunch they had a delicious ceviche in one of the gazebos which were close to the beach.
Then they looked for a place where there were no fishermen.

They found a little hotel close to the port. It was a fragile wood construction, not the cleanest place, noisy and hot but they did not care.
Anything would have done.

Nothing could stop them anymore.

After two hours in pure ecstasy they dressed and started their mountain climbing return to San Jose.

Olga had insisted Georges had to be opened; otherwise they would not have left before the next morning.

They opened the bar, stayed together and after closing Olga checked with Ernie in his hotel.

◆   ◆   ◆

When Otto next day returned from his trip to Guanacaste, Ernie had absolutely no reason to complain.
He briefed Otto about the agreements with Lappa, "Gordo" Fonseca and their agent.

Then both went in the same plane to Miami. From there they had different ways: Ernie to New York and Otto a 12 hour flight to Frankfurt.

Chapter 3
The Fight

Ernie arrived in Schenectady late Sunday night.

It was dark, snowing and very cold.

He had problems getting a rental car in Albany. When he finally had one it was already late. Then he still had to drive in bad weather.

Since he lived alone and nobody was waiting, it did not really matter.

Next day he went early to the office to prepare his written report. HH was already there. He wanted to hear Ernie's story before later getting the formal report.

He was impressed how his youngest sales manager had taken care of the business in Costa Rica and was optimistic that with Lappa and Nota on their side their chances were not bad.

After his report was finished he went to other projects and routine work always waiting to hear something from Costa Rica.

Two weeks gone, he called Lappa.

"Caldera is trying everything to keep me and my colleague Francisco Cargas out of all important matters. He is doing the evaluation of the three top ranking bids himself.

Cargas and I are working on all other bids. This keeps us busy and away from the evaluation of the bids which really matter.

Call me back after the holidays. Hopefully I have then better news."

◆   ◆   ◆

Ernie's parents had a nice home in Staten Island. It was an older house on half an acre of land, a waterfront lot with many mature trees. His father only recently had remodeled the entire house. It had a magnificent view of the Statue of Liberty and lower Manhattan.

They bought the house some twenty years ago still at a reasonable price.

In 1934 they had emigrated from the Saarland at a time when this little European heartland was still administered by France. A year later Hitler made it part of Germany. They were fortunate to be spared of all the misery Europe went through the following years.

His mother's elder brother had a chicken farm in Arkansas and had convinced them to change their life in the shade of Saarland's heavy industry for the country life on a chicken farm.

Both his father and his uncle survived the war, though his uncle with a head injury from which he never recovered. As a consequence he passed away only shortly after his return.

Since Ernie's parents never came along with his uncle's wife they left Arkansas and went to New York where his father joined the US Postal Service and his mother started a little grocery store.

In 1946 his brother Martin was born. He was killed and only 21 years old, in a traffic accident at a time when Ernie was in South Africa selling harbor cranes in the nearby Portuguese colonies Angola and Mozambique.

Ernie returned home to support his parents during these difficult times.

Then when he had a job and lived away from home, he made it a habit to always spend the holidays with his parents in Staten Island.

It was the same this year. He spent most of the time with his parents. They twice went to Manhattan by ferry. The first time they went to the theatre and the next time they saw a musical. Afterwards on their way back they stopped in little Italy and had a late dinner. It was always nice to be in New York but mostly he enjoyed being at home with his parents celebrating Christmas the old way. It made him nostalgic.

He often thought about Costa Rica, Olga, the business. He felt tempted to call Lappa before the agreed date January 3rd.

Lappa called him before that.

"Mr. Piper I have no good news.

JB has an engineer here. His name is Fred Morris. He sits in Caldera's office and is working on their bid probably making changes which is not allowed. We have a meeting in Sigul's office, where they want to explain what Morris is doing. Sigul is Caldera's boss.

Westinghouse's rep had complained with ITE's General Manager that JB has open access to our offices and to the bids.

If you are still interested in this business Mr. Piper, I urge you to personally take care of things before it is too late."

"I appreciate your call Mr. Lappa. I'll get hold of my boss. He has to make this decision. I'll call you back this evening."

Ernie called HH.

"Take the next flight and go for it. Unacceptable to rank first and being pushed out like this.

It is Argentine all over again. I would not be surprised if Maldecara is behind all this."

HH became emotional when he referred to that business which he had lost to Maldecara.

"And I am going to send Jordan Bryan with you. Nobody knows Juliano better than he does."

Ernie knew Jordan. He had served under HH in the Navy. When HH quit his service and went to GE, Jordan Bryan came with him. And when HH went to EG, again Jordan followed him. Jordan was HH's guy for special operations.

Manis with the biggest share in this project also have to do something. I will call Nova in Germany. When he hears about this he will join our forces."

Ernie liked this. This smelled like a real fight and he was a fighter. He called Lappa and gave him the news. This would also motivate Lappa.

◆   ◆   ◆

A few weeks earlier when Ernie had met with Lappa, their conversation had been overheard by David Levy, Maldecara's man for special operations in Costa Rica.

Shortly after Ernie and Lappa left the restaurant "La Cascada", he went to his nearby parked black Cadillac and drove to his little downtown office which he shared with two lawyers. He called Maldecara.

"I listened to a conversation between Piper and Lappa, one of Caldera's assistants. Lappa has committed himself to pass any information regarding the evaluation of the bids on to Piper or their agent in Costa Rica. Lappa will get a job as technical adviser with the agent who besides being agent for quite a few international corporations has the largest Ferreteria in Costa Rica."

This call finished, Maldecara didn't waste any time, calling Caldera and bringing him up to date.

Since Levy had reminded him of Piper he called his associate Sommer and asked him whether he had found out something about Piper.

"He is from New York City, only 26 years old, has a MBA degree. He spent some time in South Africa selling harbor cranes and then started working for HH on a large thermal power plant in Egypt. This is his first gas turbine project and he has no business experience in Latin America."

"So he won't bother us much. HH is not stupid; once he is aware that we have ITE on our side he won't waste his money. He might like it or not, but at some point he will back out."

◆   ◆   ◆

Caldera, Lappa and Cargas met in their boss' office.
Ing. Sigul held a little speech.

"All bids are being evaluated for their technical, commercial and legal part. Technical and commercial part is our job; the legal part is Nota's job.
I should not have to mention it, but since this is a public tender, everything is confidential. Giving information to third parties can lead to an annulment of the tender and would have severe consequences for the informant.
Ing. Caldera is in charge of the evaluation. His recommendation will be submitted to the board of directors for approval and allocation.

Ing. Caldera is free to decide what bidders may be invited to give information or clarification needed to do a proper evaluation. Without Ing. Caldera's approval no contact with bidders is allowed."

Lap got the message; this meeting was held to give him a warning and to prevent him from going his own ways.

◆   ◆   ◆

Ernie arrived the next day in San Jose and went directly to his hotel. He called the agent and told Mrs. Croman that he had come to personally take care of the business. Then he left a message at Lappa's home, asking for a meeting the same evening at Lappa's home.

This time he took a taxi cab a few blocks from his hotel and made sure that nobody followed.

Once alone with Lappa in his little home office, Lappa came immediately to the point.
He briefly reported about today's meeting and the indirect warning.
"An engineer from JB is changing part of their technical specifications in order to improve their efficiency values and their electrical output.
After these modifications JB's bid all of a sudden ranks first."

JB same as Manis were Manufacturing Associates (short MA) of General Electric. Both had offered the same equipment. So if JB made changes in their efficiency rating the consortium could do the same. Lappa's information was valuable and helpful.

Ernie was no engineer. To make technical modifications he needed somebody from Manis in Germany who manufactured the turbines.
So early next morning he called HH. HH agreed technical support was needed by Manis. So he called his colleague, Manis' president Hans Nott. Nott understood the problem and promised to immediately send his sales manager Jim Golden on his way to Costa Rica to give Ernie the support needed.
Nott needed this business badly. The manufacturing of these turbines could decide about the survival of this EG division. EG was an internationally operating group of companies with more than 300,000 employees. EG in Schenectady

and Manis Germany although independently operating belonged both to the same group.

So a business which otherwise would have been considered as average was becoming highly political. The turbine factory in Essen employed some 20,000 people. Closing this plant would have a severe impact on Germany's Ruhr region. The public and politicians were following the Costa Rica project with interest.
On Nunz' return from Costa Rica with the favorable news, about the consortium ranking first, Nott gave a press conference to inform his staff and the public worried about a closure of the plant.

The entire business could well benefit from this high motivation and public support in Germany.

◆   ◆   ◆

Jim Golden arrived two days later. A very pleasant easy going man in his mid thirties with blond hair, blue eyes and an always friendly round face. The extra pounds, which he carried with grace, suggested that he did not seriously fight life's pleasures including good food and German beer.

Ernie liked Jim the moment they met at the airport. They discussed their common business till late night. Next morning they made an official visit to ITE. Ernie introduced Wim to Caldera and the other engineers.

Jim told Caldera that his objective was to make an adjustment to the efficiency rating of the turbines, same as other MA's (not mentioning JB) had already done. GE had informed his MA's Nuovo Pignone, Manis, JB and others of the higher output.
Jim, Lappa and Ernie had come up with this story. It sounded reasonable and would fully cover Lappa.

Since Caldera had allowed JB to make these modifications he could not deny the consortium doing the same.
Caldera was perplexed, with that his protégée JB was back to zero.

Ernie left Jim at ITE, where he together with Cargas made the adjustments.

That done, they met with their agent and "El Gordo" Fonseca for lunch. El Gordo had met before with his friend Lic. Nota in his office at ITE.
Nota did not want to have any contact other than El Gordo.
He agreed to provide "legal" services from case to case. According to El Gordo, his friend Tulio was not committed to anybody but might do so at a later stage. He strongly believed in an allocation to JB.

El Gordo saw a set of all bids laying on a conference table in Nota's office.
"If any information from these documents is needed, I am sure Tulio would let me into his office to get it."

When they returned to the hotel they met Jordan Bryan who had arrived in the meantime.

Jordan with the looks of an Irish price fight boxer was no unknown to Jim. They had been in a similar competition in Argentina. It was the one HH had referred to earlier.

Jordan was the living encyclopedia in the world of gas turbines. He knew everything and everybody. It was almost scaring what details and intimacies his brain had captured. Ernie reminded himself to be careful. He had no intention to be an open book for everybody.

"Maldecara has somebody here who is following you "was one of his first observations to Ernie.

Ernie was amazed. "How do you know? You have been here less than an hour."
"Well, his name is David Levy; he used to work for the Israeli Mossad and also for the CIA. Maldecara has used him in several occasions for special operations in Latin America.
You should be very careful. Next time you go to Lappa, let me know."

"Ernie, Jordan is right, you have no idea what we went through in Argentina, "said Jim, "they had the generals on their side—all generously bribed. They did not harm us personally. But there were local people who simply disappeared."

Since it had become dark outside, it was time for the obligatory "sundowner". They went to the hotel bar.

Although Jordan had already been briefed by HH, he asked Ernie to tell him everything that had happened so far regarding this San Antonio project. He listened quietly without interrupting Ernie.

When he knew all details, he said:

"I would be surprised if Maldecara is not on his way here. He knows that Wim and I are here and that we are determined to get this business. He needs to rethink his strategy and to discuss it with Caldera and Levy."

Then he continued: "Putting myself in Juliano's shoes, what would I do and what could I do? He cannot pay bribes or promise to do so to everybody involved in this decision making. and then just wait to get the allocation.

It is not that simple.

The Worldbank is financing this. If they smell corruption, they intervene or withdraw their commitment blacklisting the country.

An allocation to JB is only sustainable if it can be proved that the JB bid is the best.

What one does in these cases? Getting the bid documents and make changes so it becomes the best bid or exchange the bid documents for new ones which are modified."

"They have three sets of these bids. Two has Caldera; one has Nota, ITE's lawyer. Whatever Caldera does is difficult to know or even to prevent.

If Nota is with them, there is little we can do.

El Gordo, Fonseca has to immediately get a copy of JB's bid from his friend Nota.

And this has to be done before Maldecara gets wind of it.

He would do everything to prevent it."

And after reflecting a moment Jordan said;" Ernie get El Gordo as soon as possible."

Ernie called El Gordo, and half an hour later El Gordo entered breathing heavy like a steam locomotive.

Ernie explained to him that they needed a complete set of JB's bid.

During bid opening every page was sealed and initialed by Lic. Nota.

So with copies sealed and initialed they always could prove if somebody had tempered with the original bid or replaced pages.

They told El Gordo that these copies were urgently needed and if in their possession tomorrow evening they would pay $ 2,000.-

El Gordo asked the bartender to pass him a telephone and then made calls for more than half an hour.

When he was finished he said:
"Tulio has a large family, 15 kids. That doesn't prevent him from having a girl friend. I was finally able to catch him with his girl friend. Therefore it took so long.
Tulio has agreed. The brother of his girl friend will pass tomorrow evening, when everybody has left, at Tulio's office to fetch the documents.
Tulio's girlfriend is of Chinese descent. Her family runs a pharmacy and is proud owner of a Xerox copy machine. The boy, his name is Lin, will take the bid documents home, make copies and bring them right away here to you. He will leave the originals with his sister who will give them tomorrow night to Tulio.
Tulio insists that in addition to the $2,000 you also should pay for the photo prints."

Ernie and Jim who also speaks perfectly Spanish translated Fonseca's proposal to Jordan.
They all agreed, had a few more drinks and went then over to Georges.

◆   ◆   ◆

Lin the 19 year old brother of Su, Nota's girlfriend, entered Nota's office exactly at 5 pm.
Nota was glad he did not wait.
"You are precise like a Swiss watch. One can rely on you. These here are the papers to copy. They are all in a box, so you can carry them on your bike. As soon as you have the copies bring them to the hotel Europa and hand them personally to Don Ernesto Piper. He will be waiting for you. They originals leave with your sister. I'll pick her up later tonight.

Lin carried the box to his delivery bike. Nobody had seen him. The building was empty. The last employees had left almost an hour ago.
That's at least what he and Nota thought.

◆   ◆   ◆

Georges did not disappoint Ernie's friends. They had met some nice girls and returned to their hotel not before the next morning.

When they met for breakfast it was already 9 am. Jordan was the last one to join them. He had already been busy.
"Juliano (Maldecara) is here. He arrived this morning and stays at the Gran Hotel. He met John Morris from JB at the airport."

"Morris is at our hotel," added Jim, "I met him on my way down. He probably just returned from the airport, picking Maldecara up. We recognized each other and said hello."

"I bet Juliano meets Calderon for lunch and proposes to let Morris work on JB's bid." predicted Morgan," Exactly what I said yesterday. Hopefully we are not too late copying Nota's set. Juliano knows how important it is that nobody has copies or even one original set of the JB bid."

They had lunch with the agent, Mrs. Croman felt left out of the game. She assured them of her support and suggested to even talk to the country's president, who had called her the day before to invite her for a social dinner if they could prove that corruption was involved.

The early evening Ernie went to visit Lappa at home to get some information about Morris' activity and the state of the evaluation.

They went in two taxis, Ernie took the first, Jordan and Jim followed and gave him cover in a second one. There were no incidents.
According to Lappa another competitor, Westinghouse, was becoming active. A Westinghouse engineer accompanied by their rep Ingeniero Sanas was in their office checking with Caldera and Sigul about the state of the evaluation.
When Ernie left Lappa's home, he walked a short distance where at the Mango tree, a cab was waiting to bring him back to the hotel. This was also a precaution to protect Lappa's reputation.

They met at the hotel bar to enjoy a few drinks and discussed the day's events.

Then all in a sudden completely out of breath, El Gordo rushed in:
"Tulio just called me, Lin the boy who was supposed to make the photo copies is missing. He left Tulio's office hours ago but did not show up at his home."

◆   ◆   ◆

After leaving Nota's office Lin loaded the heavy box with documents on his bike.
He did not pay any attention to the big dark car parking close to him and whose driver was watching him.
And if he had noticed him, he would not have cared. Nobody had told him that he was transporting sensitive papers another party had an extreme interest in.

He got on his bike and directed it towards his parents' pharmacy.

He took a shortcut through "La Cuesta Mora" a steep small valley with a narrow bridge spanning over a little river. It was an ugly dirty and this time of the day, totally dark spot which was used as garbage dump.
But he would gain more than 3 miles and that was worth it.

The dark car followed him slowly.
It had a heavy eight cylinder engine which ran quiet and smoothly.
All lights were turned off. It blended right into the dark street which was totally deserted. The ITE's employees had left some two ours ago.
Lin had no idea that he was being followed.

Lin rode with full speed down the steep slope towards the bridge in order to gain momentum for the steep way up on the other side of the bridge.
He only had eyes for the way ahead of him. The dark and unpaved road required his full attention.
When, in an angle of his eye he perceived the huge shadow of a car moving with full speed towards him it was already too late.

A shattering crash.
The impact was so solid that Lin was catapulted into the air and hitting the ground his neck broken he was dead instantly.

The cold blooded author of this intentional "accident" stopped, grasped the still intact box with the documents and threw it down the garbage dump where it most likely was washed away by the bypassing swift flowing river. .

Then without any look at the boy's body laying lifeless on the side of the road, he went to his car and speeded away.

◆   ◆   ◆

El Gordo, Jordan, Jim and Ernie were still at the hotel's bar discussing, what could have happened to Lin.

"If they get these documents before we have copies of them, given the support they have from Caldera and Sigul, they can even make a new offer."

"They can simply trash this set," continued Jordan, "Lic. Nota can never admit that his set is gone. Worse, they can even blackmail Nota to cooperate with them. He needs his set of the JB bid to do his job."

They continued discussing and speculating, when the phone rang and was passed to El Gordo. It was his friend Tulio.

"Fernando, Lin is dead. Su just called me. They found him in "La Cuesta Mora", close to the garbage dump.

He was obviously hit by a car; a hit and run, if not something worse.

So far there is no word from the box with the documents.

I will meet Su in the hospital. She and her parents are already on their way. They have to identify him.

I have to take care of Su and her parents, they need me now. I call you later at home.

Although nobody could hear what Nota said, watching El Gordo and listening to the little he said, they knew something bad had happened.

El Gordo briefed them shortly.

"Possibly it was a traffic accident, but more likely he had to die, because somebody badly wanted the set of bid documents."

Ernie suggested: "There is nothing for us to do right now. I feel bad. The boy became involved because of us. I think going to the hospital where Nota and the family meet and say that we are sorry and offer our help is the least we can do. And being there we might be able to find out what happened."

They all agreed, signed their checks and went out, to get a taxi to the hospital

They had to wait a few minutes before Nota, who had a much longer way, arrived.
Nota, who they had previously seen at the bid opening, was in his late thirties, about Ernie's height and dressed in a black suit.
He was not too happy to see his friend Fernando with three strangers.
El Gordo told him that his friends felt guilt to have Lin involved and wanted to express their condolences to Lin's family.
Finally he seemed to agree and said:
"I think it shows heart warmth and responsibility. Lin's family will understand this as a sign of solidarity."

They went inside the hospital and were led to the emergency section. Su and her parents had just identified their son and his belongings.
It was horrible, only hours ago he was with them, alive, full of youth, a promising son.

Nota explained that the four men, unknown to Lin's family, wanted to say their condolences as they also felt some guilt in what had happened.

Since in these moments of grief they hardly could ask Lin's family whether the box with the papers was among the items identified,
Jordan suggested El Gordo to ask the hospital staff who ha taken care of Lin, if such a box with documents had been registered as part of Lin's belongings.

El Gordo was able to talk to the driver of the emergency vehicle. No there had been absolutely nothing found like that.
He gave El Gordo the exact location where Lin had been found.

When El Gordo told his companions what he had learned from the driver of the emergency vehicle, they all agreed to visit the site of the accident first thing tomorrow morning.

At 7 am they met with El Gordo in the hotel's breakfast room. They took El Gordo's car and went to "Cuesta La Mora", the place where the accident had happened.

There were still some traces, dark brown spots of dried blood.
Otherwise there was nothing to see. Looking down to the little bridge and the dumpster on the left, they could well imagine what had happened and that the box was possibly thrown into the river.

"I am the lightest, why don't you let me down on a rope to the river to see if the box was dumped somewhere, down there."

◆　　◆　　◆

Maldecara had learned that Ernie Piper was back in Costa Rica. He agreed with his associate Winter, that Piper, having no experience and no support from within ITE should not represent any major problem. They had the support of the functionaries who were essential for the allocation.
Nevertheless it made him nervous, that his main competitor was still ranking first and present in person, where the decisions were made.

Since he had planned to escape the New York cold and spend the next three month in their condominium on Copacabana Beach in Rio de Janeiro, he would make a stop over in Costa Rica.
His wife and son were booked on direct flights; he took an evening flight and arrived next morning in San Jose.

On his arrival he learned from his contact David that not only Piper but also Jordan Bryan and Jim Golden were there. He knew both and was well aware that they were no novices in that kind of business.
Things started to look different. HH was obviously determined to fight. And with Jordan Bryan it became more kind of a personal issue. He and HH wanted revenge for Argentine and other businesses he had taken from them.

Golden did not concern him too much. It confirmed only that they were in a desperate situation to get the business, similar to JB.

He called Caldera and got other news he didn't like.

"I just had Golden from Manis and Piper her. Since Morris from JB changed the efficiency rates, Golden is now next door and doing the same. Golden said that they received information from their common license holder General Electric about alternative output values.

With that you and your friends from JB are back to where you were in comparison to the EG bid. In the overall ranking you overtook Westinghouse who of course is not associated with GE."

"I told you before Fernando there is a leak in your office. This alternative out put rating was nothing more than a trick to put JB ahead. GE has nothing to do with that, they used GE simply as a pretext to do the same as JB did.

I will talk to Morris. We have to find a way to get ahead of EG."

After hanging up he called Morris at the hotel and asked him to meet him to meet at the Gran Hotel.

Sitting on the hotel's terrace and sipping their cafe Maldecara told about the conversation he just had with Caldera. "All you did, the modification of the output data is for nothing. Golden from Manis is doing the same right now. He is assisted by Lappa and Cargas and by now his bid ranks first again."

"Fred, I thought about this. There is only one option left:

You have to give Caldera a reason to lower your total bid price in his evaluation.

This only can be done by changing the original bid suggesting and showing that your price was for a Cadillac where the other bidders offered a Chevrolet.

So by bringing your bid on the same level as the EG bid, your bid is, say $ 100,000 cheaper.

You have to upgrade and modify the civil part e.g. to justify your higher price, same with the mechanical part etc.> It has to add up to approximately $1 Million. Where you can not make changes of course, that's the turbines, since you are offering the same as EG.

Caldera has to give you access to your three sets of original documents. You simply exchange parts or pages in all three sets.

Let's discuss details with Caldera."

Caldera liked the idea and agreed to immediately meet with Morris to discuss the further procedure. He promised to talk to Nota in order to also get his set of documents.

Nota was in court, but he would be back the afternoon. Nota had never declined him a favor.

When he later talked to Nota, he agreed. But since he needed his set himself, Caldera could have it only the day after tomorrow. Caldera did not insist.
What did it matter, Morris had to prepare the pages which were supposed to be exchanged and would do the swapping not before two or three days.

◆   ◆   ◆

Maldecara hid his surprise, when Caldera told him about Nota's reaction. With the instinct of an old fox he sensed that something was not kosher. His contact David Levy had told him that Nota's friend El Gordo was working for Piper. And he knew the way Jordan Bryan was handling things. Bryan knew him inside-out; he had literally slipped into his skin.
Bryan probably was anticipating that his only choice left was to temper with the JB bid and that this would only work if he had all three sets and if no copies of an original set was made.

Supposing Bryan would get hold of Nota's set. He would immediately make copies and he could only do this outside the ITE premises. Photo copies had to be registered r if they were made with ITE's photo copiers—especially since they were so many. Either Nota would take them personally out of the office, or somebody would come and pick them up.
He had to have this set before anybody could make copies. The best was to get this set and simply destroy it. If Nota got it back, one could never be certain that no copies were made later or Nota could simply keep the set and use it against him.

He called David and explained his concerns.
"The best is if you watch Nota's office today.
Either tonight or tomorrow night somebody, probably Nota himself, will try to take them out of ITE's premises.
You have to get them and immediately destroy them, so nobody can use them against us."

◆   ◆   ◆

Jordan Bryan gestured to his three companions to come. He pointed to something that looked like a new carton box.

Fortunately El Gordo carried a rope in his car. Since Ernie was the lightest and most agile, they gave in to his suggestion to let him down with the rope.
He put the rope around his waist and held by his friends he started his descent through the slippery and bad smelling garbage.

Everybody was watching with excitement when he reached the box. It was intact and still had the rubber straps securing it. Ernie took the straps off. It was what they had been looking for.
After the box and Ernie were pulled up and the worst dirt removed, they put the box into El Gordo's car.

"Now let's discuss what to do next," suggested Jordan.
"Nobody knows whether this was just a traffic accident and it is impossible to prove that Lin was killed, to get and dump these documents. Although we have an idea who might have an interest in this, it does not prove anything.
So we probably gain nothing if we turn this matter over to the police."

"The police here are not used to handling matters that complicated," agreed El Gordo.
"They are going to treat this as simple traffic accident.
Involving the police could be counterproductive.
If we argue that there is the only one party interested in possessing these documents, it is easy enough to prove that we are the other party benefiting at least as much having them.
It would much to hurt Nota who gave us access to these papers."

Everybody admired El Gordo's logical reasoning and agreed to leave things as they were. After making the copies, they would return the bid documents to Nota's office.

"I wonder what happens when Juliano becomes aware, that Nota still has his set. By the way he did not order murder nor did he intentionally cause this accident. He has never done anything like that."

They went to a Xerox shop made the copies and the same morning El Gordo visited Nota in his office putting the heavy box on the conference table.

"Julio we found the documents. They had been trashed close to the location where Lin died. The EG guys have already made one set of prints.
Jim gave me the money we agreed on. I am not taking anything. I give my part to Lin's family."

"Oh Fernando I can not tell you how relieved I am.
But this entire matter should be handed over to the police. If this was intentional I want the murderer to be prosecuted."

Fernando explained him what they had contemplated and discussed. Nota finally agreed. He was lawyer. He knew better than his friend how right they were.

◆   ◆   ◆

The engineers including Caldera never came to know of the previous incident. Caldera was angry with Nota who contrary to his promise refused to give him his set of documents.

Maldecara had already left for Brazil to join his family.
David his Central American contact had confirmed that the documents did not exist anymore. He kept it to himself how he got them and what he had done with them.

Caldera finally decided to recommend JB for allocation to the board of directors. Morris was able to change the civil part and mechanical part in such a way that if ITE would ever take it, they would get a palace instead of the power station they had tendered for.
Of course this was all a fake to justify JB's higher bid price.
The respective pages had been exchanged, but only in the two sets which were with the engineers.
Nota's set was they only one nobody had tampered with.

It was now Caldera's evaluation job to give JB credit for the "palace" and the "de luxe" mechanics in order to bring the evaluated price under that of EG.

What finally would be built, that was again in his hands since he was responsible for this project till it was handed over turn key; an almost perfect manipulation of the tender documents to benefit the bidder he was committed to.

He was the only one having access to both, the JB and the EG bid. His assistants were handling the bids of those who already had been discarded.

Nevertheless he was well aware; there was still the original bid which Nota had.

But he did not worry too much about Nota. Somehow he would come to an arrangement with him.

What he did not have the slightest idea of was, that the EG consortium had made copies of Nota's set.

Caldera gave instructions to Lappa and Cargas to have their evaluation ready in one week from now. Nota had already handed him his report regarding all legal observations and objections as well as counter proposals made by the bidders.

Based on these reports and the commercial evaluation, which was the summary of all single reports expressed in money terms, he would prepare his recommendation for the "Junta Directiva".

He counted on support of his direct superior, Jorge Sigul and the corporation's president Andy Quarry. The general manager of the Instituto Ticaraguanese de Electricidad (ITE), Juarez Tejido was neutral. If his recommendation was founded Juarez would not object.

In two weeks it would be all over. He could look forward to soon be a wealthy man; and belonging to the family of one of Costa Rica's most influential presidents, he had the money he needed for his political career.

◆   ◆   ◆

Lappa was well aware that the evaluation was soon coming to an end. His boss had made it clear, he would favor JB. When Ernie called him for another meeting at his home, he agreed to meet next day.

They met; Ernie's trip by taxi was again closely watched by Jordan and Jim who followed in a second cab.

Lappa reported that JB's Fred Morris had been around some time, always locked in Caldera's office.

According to his boss, JB had offered a civil part and mechanical part which was by far exaggerated. So he was discussing with Morris other options to bring their price down.

Offering the same standard as offered by EG, the JB bid was $100,000 less than the one presented by EG.

Accepting the higher standards JB had offered, they would get credit, which again would put them ahead of the EG consortium.

So Caldera did not make it a secret, he would recommend JB for allocation.

When Ernie met with Jim and Jordan and gave them the news, he had the feeling that Jordan who up to this moment was the driving force behind their common cause had lost interest.

Jordan had given him such a sense of security and his sober analytic way of seeing and solving problems had not only energized him but also contributed to the optimism so badly needed in situations like these.

When he was alone for a moment with Jim, he asked him about this sudden change in Jordan's attitude.

"Jordan has problems at home." answered Jim, "his wife Mary is not easy. I know her; I spent some days at his home. When Jordan is away from her he is a great guy. In Mary's presence he is tame and docile like a lamb. They are both very jealous. He has been away for too long.

He is becoming aware, that this business is much more complicated and time consuming than he anticipated.

I have the impression he is looking for an excuse to get out as a pretext to declare this a lost cause."

Ernie was aware that their front was becoming brittle.

If Jordan wanted back, he could not stop him. Before he was here, Ernie had done pretty well and without Jordan he could do things his way.

Despite all his undeniable assets Jordan had the mentality of Irish cop;—not always the optimal way to solve problems in Latin America.

Nevertheless, he was good in handling guys like Maldecara and Levy.

Ernie had adapted much better to the Latin mentality and was able to turn disadvantages rapidly into advantages. He was flexible, quick and able to motivate—even manipulate the Ticos.

Ernie was concerned that Jordan in need of an excuse for abandoning this business would simply declare it a lost cause.
As a consequence, HH on whom he had great influence was likely to withdraw his support and call Ernie home.
All that at a time when things were problematic, but far from being lost.

Something dramatic had to be done to motivate their brittle front:
Lappa, Nota, their agent, HH, Golden and last himself.

Jordan had gone to his room. He was packing and leaving the next morning. That was quick.
Jim went to Georges.
Ernie was in no mood for anything but to find a solution for this imminent problem. He was laying on his bed and staring at the ceiling.
And then he had an idea.

He called Jim in his room. Jim had just returned.

"Jim I need to talk to you, can I come over?"

He went next door. Jim was already in his bed.

"I have been thinking all evening about our situation. If we do not do something dramatic, this business will go down the drain. We are loosing momentum. Nobody stands behind this anymore. Jordan is leaving, we have neither Lappa's nor Nota's support. El Gordo works for the agent and the agent was never really committed.
It is not that I am painting a black picture because I am in a pessimistic mood. Contrary I want to be constructive and just highlight the facts so we know where we are, in order to do the next important step.

If you return without an order there will be major problems for the entire gas turbine division. The factory will be closed and thousands of people will lose their job.

We need a high level intervention to prevent the engineers from doing what they are planning to do.

Being able to prove that the evaluation and subsequent recommendation for allocation is based on a bid which has been modified after bid opening, we have a case where the agent has offered to talk to president Jepe.

With the president's intervention before the board has come to a decision, we have a good chance that an allocation is done the proper way.

However, once the board has allocated this project and it is published in La Gaceta it will be almost impossible to find somebody to support our cause.

That is why we have an agent and why he gets a million dollar commission. It is his (or her) job to get whoever is needed to intervene, so everything can take its proper course."

Jim agreed to ask the agent, Mrs. Croman to immediately contact and brief president Jepe in order to intervene with Andy Quarry, ITE's president, before a recommendation was given to the Junta Directiva.

They met Mrs Croman at her home and when they finally convinced her to call the Casa Presidential, she was informed that the president was touring the country's Northern provinces. It would be impossible to get an audience before the next two weeks.

They thanked Mrs. Croman for at least trying.

When they returned to the hotel, they ran into Fred Morris from JB.

Morris gave them a friendly hello, pointing his thumb upwards, the old Caesarian sign which decided upon life or death of the gladiators.

Most probably Morris did not think in these historic terms, he just wanted to indicate that his matters were in best shape.

Jim and Ernie honestly envied him.

It was all so frustrating. The right was on their side.

Whatever they did it didn't work.

Everybody was getting tired, no more motivation.

Lappa, Nota and the agent they often did not even return their calls.

Absolutely different was their competitor's situation.

ITE's functionaries, who had the say, favored JB and pushed JB by all means.

Maldecara's seed was flourishing.

Whatever way Ernie tried to look at it, an intervention of the country's president seemed to be the only way to prevent an allocation to their competitor. And only something spectacular like this was necessary to keep his troops together.
Almost certain that Nota and Lappa already thought of changing fronts to at least benefit with a little of the generous bribes which were paid. An occasion like this one did not occur every year.

HH could call him back any moment. Only if he was able to convince HH that they still had a realistic chance, would he be allowed to continue his fight.

He was literally fighting on three fronts.

What could he Ernie a 26 year old foreign salesman do, to get the president of this country to do, what he him wanted to do.

After dinner they went to Georges. He had not seen Olga for a few days and badly needed some distraction. She was beautiful as ever. He had a nice time chatting with her and had a few drinks. But he was in no mood to wait for her till 3 am when she was closing the bar. So not long after midnight Jim and he went back to their hotel. They were again discussing their problems.

"Listen Jim, perhaps I have a solution. It is a little farfetched, but never mind. I need you to answer some questions."
"Do your people in Germany still believe we get this business?"
"Affirmative!"

"What would happen, if they learn that the business goes to JB?"

"We immediately would have to stop production, and lay off hundreds of production personnel. This would cause uproar. The union would call for solidarity strikes and demos."

"Don't you have a socialistic government now?"

"No not socialistic but social democratic, in the States you would say liberal. Willy Brandt its leader is now chancellor or head of government."

"Never mind, liberal or whatsoever. This Willy Brandt is he not supported by the unions or better yet, does he not owe his chancellorship to the unions?"

"That is exactly correct. He and the unions are in one bed."

"Does your factory have influential union people?"

"Oh yes Ernie. That has been our problem all the time. That is the reason we are not able to rationalize our production and improve our productivity the way we would like to. Our union people are the ones who have the saying."
"To make it short the same people who have a vital interest in this business and in your company have a strong influence on your government."
"I have heard the agent say that the German government is very involved in Costa Rica. The ruling party here, "Liberacion" is financed by the ruling party in Germany. This Willy Brandt is the head of this international socialistic or as you said social democratic movement."

"Jim why don't we call now, this very moment one of your union people and tell him how things here really are:
We rank first. Our competitor has bribed the entire utility company which is owned by the state. We want the country's president to intervene and make sure that the allocation is done the proper way.
We want a top person from the German government to contact this president here and ask him to give us an audience as soon as possible so we can explain with our own words what is going on."

"Ernie it is the craziest idea I have ever heard; but it might work.
Besides I agree with you, we have no choice, either now or never; and it also works for me.
With that the ball is in their (the union's) court.
Germany is 7 hours ahead of us, I will get Mr. Graboski during his breakfast time."

Only moments later Jim was talking to the union's leader in Essen, Mr. Graboski.

He explained in very short words as Ernie had suggested.
Graboski felt flattered.
Receiving a phone call from the other side of the world from the director of sales, asking him to save the factory and the jobs of all its workers, to help him with such an important business which otherwise was lost.

He promised to immediately call Professor Horst Ehmke, Willy Brandt's chief of staff.
Jim and Ernie felt, they finally had done something positive and went to bed.
It was 3 am.

Chapter 4
Willy Brandt
German Chancellor
and
Don Jepe
President of Costa Rica

It was just before 7 am when Jim's telephone rang.

"I am Heiko Froehlich, delegate of the Friedrich Ebert Stiftung. We are part of the German Social Democratic Party. I am in charge of the party's activities in Central America."

Jim had heard of these so called "secret ambassadors" Their activities were not limited or influenced by diplomatic protocols. They were often used by the ruling parties for unofficial and sometimes delicate missions.

"I received a telex from Willy Brandt, our head of government. I am supposed to show you this telex and pass it immediately to president Jepe.

I would appreciate if we could meet at our office as soon as possible.

We are on the 7th floor of the McDonalds building opposite of the Central Bank."

Jim called Ernie who was still asleep.

"Your crazy idea was not so crazy after all. Brandt has really sent a telex which we are supposed to see before it is passed to president Jepe."

Jim told Ernie about the phone call from the Ebert foundation.

"I never thought that German political parties have "secret ambassadors" in this country.

Ernie, hurry—I can't wait to see what you stirred up with your crazy idea."

They had a quick breakfast and then went over to the McDonalds building to meet Froehlich.

"I did not know that Manis has such important business in Costa Rica; that Brandt himself gets involved.
This morning 5 am, I received a call from the chancellor's office asking me to check my telex for an urgent message from Willy Brandt to the Ticaraguan president.
Here it is. Read it yourselves.

◆   ◆   ◆

Graboski, member of the German Social Democratic Party since the late twenties, prosecuted as such during the Third Reich and union member since the reestablishment of unions in Germany after the war. He was the elected spokesperson of his union comrades. If something had to be done in the interest of his comrades or the union he would fight for it. When his union comrades had a problem they could rely on him. He was the seventh child of polish immigrants who came in the early 1920th to the Ruhrarea in Germany to work in the coal mines.
Many comrades in the labor movement had a similar background.

Graboski knew that this power also implied a great responsibility. The twenty thousand workers and their families who depended on their jobs with the Manis turbine factory expected from him not only aggressive slogans and speeches typical for the unions. They wanted to keep these jobs and they expected him to fight for their interests.

Since most of the politicians of the ruling party came from the labor movement even the management of the turbine division relied on him.

He had promised to help, and he keeps his promises. He had a good relationship with Professor Horst Ehmke, chief of staff of Brandt's cabinet. Ehmke had his electoral mandate in Essen and knew about the critical situation of the factory.

Graboski dialed Ehmke's secret direct number and a moment later Ehmke was on the other end of the line:

"Horst you are aware about the situation in our works. For the time being the labor problem could be solved if we get the manufacturing of four turbines which are part of a deal with the Ticaraguan government. It is a public tender financed by the Worldbank.

Having offered the lowest price we officially rank first.

Our sales manager is in Costa Rica and just called me. He informed me that, some key players within the government owned utility company have been bribed by a competitor and are stealing their allocation.

He needs a clear message to the country's president to intervene."

"Eugen," that was Groboski's first name, "you know I am always here for my friends and comrades who supported me. If the people in Essen had not voted for me, I would not be here.

We support the Ticaraguan government and the ruling party "Liberacion". The president's electoral campaign was largely financed by us. Through the Friedrich Ebert Foundation we are establishing their union movement and are training workers to become efficient union leaders. The training center "La Catalina" totally financed by the Friedrich Ebert foundation is the back bone of "Liberacion".

Ehmke was university professor and as such had a encyclopedia like knowledge of everything concerning the government and its politics.

"I am with the Chancellor in about 15 minutes. Be assured I will take this matter up with him. Call me back before lunch time."

When Graboski called Ehmke before taking his lunch break, Ehmke read him the telex which already had been transmitted to the party's office in Costa Rica.

◆　　　◆　　　◆

Quote:
Note for Mr. Froehlich: please submit this telex immediately to the president.

His Excellency
Sr. Don Jepe
President of Costa Rica

Estimated Sr. President, dear colleague,

I have learned that the German company Manis participates in a public tender for an electric power station. Officials from Manis are presently in your country awaiting the outcome of this tender.
It would be appreciated if you could receive them for an audience.

Dear Mr. President let me assure you, a favorable consideration of the Manis bid would be seen as a further sign of good relationship between our two countries.

Willy Brandt
Chancellor of the Federal Republic of Germany unquote

That was by far more than Jim and Ernie had expected and hoped for.

Ernie had to admit, he felt proud. He had masterminded this. A little nobody had initiated a communication between two heads of state. One of the world leading politicians was promoting his cause.
And this was no fiction, fantasy—it was real.

Until yesterday this was his own, his very private idea. He had put figures into this game and so far he was playing them quite successfully:
The union spokesman Graboski, the chief of staff of the German cabinet Prof. Ehmke, the German head of state Willy Brandt and Don Jepe the president of Costa Rica.

His thoughts were interrupted by Heiko Froehlich: "So far I could not get hold of the president. He is in Guanacaste. The secretary general of the party is trying to contact him by radio. As soon as he is able to speak to the president he will call me.
They take this telex from Brandt serious."

He made a pause. After a while he animated Jim and Ernie: "But now tell me something about this famous business of yours. I am very interested. I never had to deal with international tenders. I studied politics and sociology. I set up the educational center La Catalina to train Central American workers to start their own labor movement, their own unions."

Jim told in a short form what so far had happened.
For Froehlich this was an unknown world. He was a teacher in whose world was no room for dirty business practices.

Ernie and Jim left after a while and went back to the hotel. Froehlich had promised to contact them as soon as he had news.

When they entered the hotel lobby, they met Fred Morris. He was friendly as always and made his obligatory "thumbs up" sign.
This time Jim and Ernie were laughing and returned the provoking salute.
When they turned back, they saw a perplexed looking Morris shaking his head, certainly wondering what kind of good news his competitors had received.
Jim and Ernie remained in the lobby had coffee and some pastry, when the operator Sandra called them over the loud speaker.

It was Froehlich. He had a message from the secretary general. He finally had been able to talk to the president by radio. The president was already on his way back and would be in San Jose in the late afternoon.
Although the telex had not been read to him, he had learned that the German Chancellor had asked for an audience for two foreign business men.

Being a personal request from Willy Brandt, it had to be taken care of.
So through the secretary general he extended an invitation to Jim and Ernie to visit him this evening for supper in his Curriadabat residence.

Ernie and Jim had what they wanted.

"Let's give the agent a call," suggested Ernie, "now we can show her that one can well move things in this country."

They called Mrs. Croman and were surprised how insistent she demanded to accompany them to the president's home.
"After all I am your agent."

Jim suggested: "Let's do her that favor, if this means so much to her. But she has to call the president's residence and tell them that there is one diner more."

They passed their day relaxing and enjoying the idea of playing international politics. They had agreed the agent would pick them up 6.15 pm at the hotel. The audience was set for 7 pm.

As usual on time the chauffeur driven white Mercedes stopped in front of the hotel. Mrs. Croman was elegantly dressed and obviously a little excited.
Ernie who had briefly seen the president after the Lanica hijacking remembered that he was about her age and an attractive looking man.

They arrived a little early and decided to wait a few minutes in the close by Curriadabat neighborhood. In Costa Rica it is ok if one is an hour late, the usual "hora Tica" however, it is considered impolite to be early and embarrass the host who might not yet be ready for his guests.

A little after seven they drove to the residence gate which was opened by a casually dressed guard.

The president expected them on the outside steps leading to his home.

He was dressed in a light blue Guayabera dark pants and sparkling black shoes. He was about 5 1/2 foot with the slim trained figure of a long distance runner. His pronounced features, prominent chin and thin hawk like nose were visible signs of his strong will power.
Wrinkles around his eyes suggested more a sense of humor and that he liked laughing than that he was already in the late fifties.

Standing there alone on the stairs of his house he looked more like a lonely bachelor welcoming some family members than what one would expect a president to look like.
This was the famous Don Jepe who had completely reshaped his country. His uncommon ideas had made him a legend during lifetime.
He was the first leader in America who had totally abolished military.
The country's welfare system was one of the most advanced of all developing countries.
Money others spend for military was invested in education; illiteracy was with less than two percent the lowest in America.

The leader of this wonderful country greeted them in fact like relatives he had not seen for a while.

Mrs. Croman, who he called with certain tenderness "Irmita", using the diminutive of her first name Irma, received two besitos—kisses—on her thickly powdered cheeks.
Ernie who he took for German, received his nickname "El Alemancito" and when they later in numerous occasions met, he always called Ernie by that name and he never forgot how he met "El Alemancito" the first time.
Jim was the botanist, due to his hobby as collector of orchids.

Don Jepe, how the president was called by his people, the Ticos, led his guests into a large room which was furnished with blue velvet sofas and easy chairs of the same color. Later when they were more acquainted he told them that this furniture was a gift from President J. F. Kennedy.

He invited them to take seats and feel at home. Two young girls served "bocas", delicious appetizers. The president asked them for their drinking preferences and then personally mixed and served them Scotch whisky.

After that they chatted about everything, his trips to Germany, some jokes and Ernie could not resist mentioning that they actually had already briefly met him during the hijacking of the Lanica plane where he personally had led the successful attack.
He laughed and said: "once a guerrillero always a guerrillero."

Then after more than an hour the president made reference to the telex which Mr. Froehlich, shortly before they arrived, had brought to his home.
"This San Antonio project is of vital importance for our country.
During the raining season, a period of approximately seven months, we receive our electric power from hydroelectric power stations. During the dry season which is very pronounced and lasts between 5 and 6 month the water reserves collected in artificial reservoirs are being used up faster each year. Demand for electric power has risen dramatically.

To compensate for the shortage of water during the peak months of the dry season, from February to May, we need additional sources to produce the energy required.

Therefore generating electric power during the peak month of the dry season with gas turbines is of vital importance for our country. We highly appreciate that the Worldbank finances this project with a long term credit at favorable conditions.

The executive president of ITE, Don Andy Quarry, is in charge of this project. ITE although owned by the state is an autonomous institution.

Don Andy and his qualified staff of engineers together with "la junta directiva' the board of directors will decide which of all the offers received is the best for our country.

I have no influence on the outcome of this temder."

With that he concluded his discourse.

"And now let's have something to eat. I like German food; it is hearty, sometimes a little heavy for the evening. Well let's see what the cook has prepared for us. Ah it looks like Stroganoff; she usually does that very well."

He was talking and talking. Ernie was becoming impatient. Never mind the rules of politeness at a presidential dinner table, if he did not make his point very soon, this would be a missed opportunity.

"Excuse me Mr. President," he interrupted the pleasant and relaxing atmosphere, "since you gave us the honor of being your guests, I feel obliged to clarify some points, and otherwise you might get the wrong impression of the purpose of our visit.

Mr. Froehlich had instructions to read us the telex which the German chancellor had directed to you. This telex was written with the best intentions but without knowledge of the situation. Therefore we asked for this audience to give you details of our concerns.

Mr. President we have duly submitted the technically best offer with by far the lowest price. No competitor has offered a shorter time of delivery.

In any public tender this means that we will be the allocated bidder.

That is the purpose of public tendering. The client as well as the bidder have to strictly adhere to the rules of the tender.

The advantage for both: The client gets the most favorable offer and the bidder can be sure, that if he has the best offer, he gets the business.

Everything is public; there are no secrets or personal preferences of functionaries or politicians.

It is always condition for a Worldbank financing that there is a public tender which has to be approved by the Worldbank.

We asked for this audience, because there is substantial doubt whether ITE's functionaries are respecting the rule of international public tendering.
We are deeply concerned that corruption will prevent us from being allocated.
I say this in a rather diplomatic way to leave room to correct the situation.
Mr President I would not dare to ask you for anything that is not in the best interest of your country. If bribery is involved, then servants of this country enrich themselves with the money of the people.
At the end it's not a corrupt bidder or the Worldbank, it's the people of this country that pay their corrupt public servants."

The pleasant atmosphere was gone.

The president could barely hide his anger.

"In this country and government we have no corruption or bribery. I put my hand in fire for Mr. Quarry. If this is what you fear, do not worry.
If your offer is the best, you will be allocated."

"Don Jepe that is exactly what I have been telling them all the time."
Irmita (Mrs. Croman) hurried to repair Ernie's faux pas. This is not Nicaragua or Panama. In Costa Rica there is no corruption"

"Irmita, this is so typical for these gringos, South of Rio Grande is South America, everybody there lies, steals and speaks Spanish."

With diplomatic skill, humor and jokes about the Gringos and the Germans in particular the president was able to bring the friendly and relaxing atmosphere back.
One of his jokes was the supposed name of a German lake "Retirense(e)" which in Spanish meant: "It is about time you left."

They finished the supper audience with traditional tintos and were then led out by Don Jepe as friendly and warm as he had welcomed them.

Jim and Irmita were optimistic that with Don Jepe's support everything would work out for them.

Ernie blamed himself that he with his insistence had spoiled this special evening. But on the other hand had everyone to admit that the purpose of their audience was to bring their concern to the president's attention and ask him to interfere and see that everything went right.

Well, there was still the "junta directiva" who actually did the allocation.

He would get as much information about the members and visit as many as possible. Wherever it made sense he would express his concerns.

Early next morning HH called him.

"What's the situation in sunny South America? You seem to like it there. When do you come back? What Jordan told me you are very committed, though he thinks it's a lost cause."

Ernie told him about the involvement of the German government and their audience with the president.

HH sounded impressed.

"You are really fighting for it. I like this. What are you planning next?"

"I am going to find out about the board members, their political affiliation, what influence each one usually takes when it comes to decisions. Knowing all that I will do some lobbying."

"OK Ernie good luck. From what you are saying the allocation is within 10 days. So I expect you back in the second week of February. But don't come without an order."

◆   ◆   ◆

Ernie called the agent and asked for names, phone numbers and all other information available of each board member.

President of the board was Don Eli Sala, according to the agent a distinguished gentleman in his late seventies. Un caballero, absolutely loyal to his principles honest and sincere. He was the president of the Banco Nacional, the country's largest bank..

The secretary of the board was Lic. Enrique Guzman a lawyer in charge of the legal department of the Banco Anglo. Lic. Guzman was at the same time the agent's lawyer.

Vice president of the board was Don Javier Quiro, importer of Toyota motor cars, the largest car dealership in Costa Rica.

The other six members were all well known business people or high ranking public servants. They usually followed the lead of the board's president and vice president.

Since Lic. Guzman was also Mrs. Croman's lawyer, she had no problem to arrange a lunch meeting for Ernie.
Guzman came formally dressed in a dark blue business suit. He was in his mid thirties.
Being the agent's lawyer Ernie could quickly come to the point and openly explain what kind of problems they had.
"Mr. Guzman the engineer who will recommend the bidder for allocation is bribed. We informed president Figueres about this situation. Now we are looking for support from members of the board of directors."

"As long as I am with the board, the members of the board have never objected recommendations from the engineering department. If your competitor has these people on his side, bad for you."

"But if your allegations are true, then nobody should allow that a bidder who bribes public servants becomes the beneficiary of his criminal actions.
I shall arrange a meeting with Don Eli Sala. He definitely has to know this, and so has Don Javier Quiro. Don Eli is neither a partisan of the president nor of Don Andy Quarry.
Today it is Friday; the board comes together Tuesday in one week. We have to rush things, to inform and convince the board members that this time they should not simply accept the recommendation submitted by the engineers."

When Ernie returned to the hotel, he had two messages waiting. One was from El Gordo, who asked for his immediate call and the other one from Lappa suggesting a meeting in his home at 7 pm.

El Gordo wanted to meet urgently at the hotel. He arrived only a few minutes later. He looked as if he had important news.

◆   ◆   ◆

A couple hours earlier there had been a meeting in Sigul's office. Subject was the presentation of both technical and legal report, the evaluation report.
They were all there: Caldera, Lappa, Cargas, Sigul and Nota.

Nota started commenting his legal expertise.
"Since we agreed to limit the legal work to the three top ranking bidders, I start with the EG consortium whose bid has the lowest price."
Sigul interrupted:
"According to Ing. Caldera if the same standards are applied for the civil and mechanical part, the JB bid is more than $100,000 lower than EG."
Caldera went red and pale. That was the last he had wanted, an open discussion about this issue now. Why couldn't Sigul just shut up?

Nota enjoyed the situation. That's what he had planned. He had suggested this meeting and an open discussion about everyone's job.

"Well this is new to me," said Nota showing his surprise,
"Since I have a complete set of these three bids, I was so free and checked the scope of delivery including civil and mechanical part and to me the offers from EG and JB are identical both strictly adhering to the tender specification.
The same goes for Westinghouse, only that their turbines naturally are not GE but Westinghouse.

Unless we have different bids (mines are the original ones duly sealed and initialed) there should not be a problem and one does not have to be an engineer. to do these comparisons.
Everybody who can add numbers can do that."

"Lic. Nota there is no need to have this kind of discussion. Your job is the legal part and not to discredit what my engineers have done."

"Ing. Sigul as syndicus of this corporation and head of its legal department it is also my job to see that this public tender is handled the proper way. I would rather see what you are talking about and why JB all in a sudden ranks first."

Nota did not know what exactly had lead to Lin's death.
But he was certain that one way or the other those who were so desperately pushing the JB bid had something to do with it.
He was determined not to make it that easy for them.

Caldera knew, it was about time for him to say something
"Tulio (Nota's first name), what you are saying are severe allegations."

"Oh Fernando (Caldera's first name), I thought you had lost you voice. I was waiting to hear from you. No these are not allegations; but if you do not explain yourself ...
You are free to do your own interpretations.
If you prefer that we talk this over, you and I that might be the best."

Caldera nodded his head. He was obviously relieved to have this subject removed.

Nota enjoyed mastering the situation. He cleared his voice and continued:

"Let me tell you about the legal work I did:

First EG:
-they agree to delivery and construction time
-they agree to penalty on late delivery
-they object to payment of indemnities for consequential damages
Their objection is reasonable; their further proposals concerning the legal part can be negotiated.

Second JB:
-they do not agree to penalty for delay.
This alone is sufficient to reject their offer. In other words none of their quoted delivery times is binding. If there is a delay it will be without consequences for them.
Nota continued with the two next ranking bidders and then went to his office waiting for Caldera. He did not wait long.

"Tulio why did you make these accusations in front of my subordinates and Ing. Sigul?"

"Fernando you have yourself committed to very dangerous people. When you asked me to give you my set of the JB bid, EG figured that part of the JB offer was going to be replaced.
The fight for that set of original documents led to the death of a good friend of mine."

◆   ◆   ◆

Caldera called Maldecara in Brazil who in turn contacted David Levy only to confirm that Nota's allegations were correct.

"I had no idea what was done to prevent EG from getting the bid documents. I am terribly sorry and although Levy assured me, that it was an accident, I no longer will use his services.
Any news from your competitors?"

"They were with the president and without naming anybody accused ITE of bending to corruption. The president called Quarry and warned him, if any of EG's accusations would prove correct, that he had to bear the consequences."

"So the fight is really on. Do you foresee any problems with the allocation?"

"Not under normal circumstances, though I don't no what other surprises these guys have. So far the junta directiva never objected our recommendations."
"Anything I can do, "asked Maldecara

"Well, for the moment stay away from our country. I will submit my recommendation for the junta session next Tuesday. Call me Wednesday."

◆   ◆   ◆

Ernie invited El Gordo to his room, anticipating important news.

"I just talked to Nota," started El Gordo, "we cannot count on him anymore. He came to an agreement with Caldera, financially I mean.

There was a confrontation in Siguls office. Nota and Caldera met afterwards and came to an arrangement.
I am sorry, but that's the way Nota is.
What do you plan now?"

"Well things are not bad. Quarry, the engineers and even the president are warned. They all know, we are committed to fight for our right and that our actions are not easy to predict. We have our own ways.
Even if they get JB allocated, it would not be the end.
We would just go to the next battle."

Ernie did this tough talk on purpose.
First, he wanted to encourage and motivate the few people who were still with him.
Second, he wanted to scare his opponents. El Gordo certainly would talk to his friend Tulio Nota and Nota would inform Caldera and so on.

After El Gordo had left, he called Olga. He asked her to join him for dinner.
After the meeting with Lappa he wanted to forget about this business and simply relax in her company.
All the ups and downs he had gone through the last 48 hours, it was more than he could bear.

Olga accepted. She was going to ask a friend to take her place in the bar and also open and close it for her.

Jim who previously had met with Froehlich from the Ebert foundation, wanted to accompany Ernie to Lappa's home.

Lappa lead them into his library and home office and reported the days events: Apart from the heated discussion in Sigul's office, he mentioned that Quarry came personally to their department and had a long conversation with Caldera behind closed doors. At the same time Lappa took twice a call from a Mr. Maldecara, who to his knowledge was related to JB.
Lappa continued telling the days history, but there was nothing new. He said that within ITE it was well known, that not only Caldera and Sigul but also Andy Quarry, ITE's president strongly favored JB.

The big question was now, would Ernie succeed in winning the support of the Junta members. They after all had the final saying.

Lappa accompanied them to the iron gate, waiting till the taxi had passed the mango tree. He was alone; his wife was visiting a friend and would not be back for at least an hour.
To demonstrate that he was not supporting a loosing team, Ernie told him on the way out about their audience with president Figueres.

"This is probably why big boss Don Andy spent today so much time in Caldera's office."

Having learned about the president's involvement, Lappa felt much better. He pulled the heavy iron gate and had it almost closed when like grown from the dark, two phantom-like figures dressed in dark sport outfits and wearing sunglasses pushed him forward and forced their way into Lappa's property. One covered Lappa's head with a linen bag. Then they started punching and kicking him carefully avoiding hitting his head or causing him any kind of visible injuries. Not a single word was spoken. This was no doubt a professional job somebody had ordered. They continued working Lappa's soft parts even when he was already unconsciously laying on the entrance floor of his house.

All this lasted not more than a few minutes. The two phantoms took the bag from his head and then left the property not touching anything.

When Lappa's wife returned she found her husband still without any sign of life, the same way the intruders had left him.

Not seeing any sign of violence, she thought her husband had suffered a stroke or for some other natural reason had become unconscious.
She called an ambulance who rushed the still unconscious to the nearest hospital. Only there the physician on duty detected the bruises and internal injuries from which Lappa was suffering. Lappa slowly regained conscience but it took him a while to remember what had happened.

When x-rays and ultra sonic tests were made the next day it became clear that his liver and kidneys were badly hurt by the violent assault.
For the next weeks Lappa would be unable to return to his job.

When Ernie and Jim heard from Mrs. Lappa that obviously immediately after they had left her husband, he had been assaulted and badly beaten up, their first reaction was to bring this to the president's knowledge—just to show how justified Ernie's concerns were.

They quickly discarded that idea, which would have uncovered their source of information. This could have caused real problems for Lappa.

The attack on Lappa, whoever was responsible for it, had been well planned. There was really nothing they could do. Their flow of information from the engineering department was stopped. This in addition to Nota's changing fronts left them without any friendly connection to ITE.

The only informant and support was Lic. Guzman whose job as secretary of the Junta was to prepare the next session and coordinate everything needed for an allocation of this tender by the junta.

Necessarily all information had to come to him.

◆   ◆   ◆

The evening before, after their meeting with Lappa, when they returned to the city, Ernie saw Olga's Land Rover already waiting in front of the hotel.
Le left Jim on his own and entered Olga's vehicle.

Dressed in an elegant black silk dress, which accentuated her sensual formed body, exposing just a little of her beautifully formed firm breasts, she would have been a more adequate decor for Mrs. Croman's Mercedes.
Ernie too was already dressed for an elegant dinner event.

They kissed long and passionately.
"I am starving for some real good food.
Where do you want me to direct my expedition vehicle?" asked Olga.

"I made a reservation in the Casino Espanol; they serve real gourmet dinner and prepare a lobster flambee al whisky which is a culinary experience. The owner and chef is Catalan form Barcelona. He is a nice guy and can tell stories from all parts of the world."

There were not many guests in the restaurant. Rodrigo the chef welcomed Ernie and Olga like old friends and gave them a nice table between large tropical plants. The sound of Spanish music, the dimmed light and the nicely decorated table created a pleasant and cozy atmosphere.

A candle was lit and Ernie ordered two La Ina's, dry Sherry's from Jerez de la Frontera in Spain. It was their first time together in a civilized and cultivated ambience. And they enjoyed it.

They ordered salad of palmitos and the famous langosta al whisky. Olga selected a bottle of white Rioja, a wine which went good with the food they had ordered. They sat opposite to each other, Olga took Ernie's hand, their eyes met, they were happy.

The food was superb; they talked about their past, their future, and their plans. They came to know each other.

The atmosphere totally different of course than Georges, the little out hang where men and girls met was much more adequate to create the kind of relationship each one had expected.

They concluded their dinner with the traditional tinto and a Carlos V, the famous Spanish brandy.

Olga invited Ernie to her home. She lived together with her father in a nice neighborhood in the west of the city. Her father was at the annual meeting of the communist party in La Havana, Cuba.

Olga showed him the house. It was furnished with old heavy wood pieces, several oil paintings and many framed photos showing her father with all famous communist leaders. There was Manuel Mara with Stalin, with Chruchtshow and of course several times with his friend Fidel Castro.

They went into her bedroom.
They slowly undressed each other.
They enjoyed looking at their bodies; they made love.
All problems were forgotten.

The birds were already singing and the new day was starting when Ernie called for a taxi cab to bring him back to the hotel.

◆   ◆   ◆

A message from Guzman was waiting for him. They had a meeting with Don Eli Sala at the Banco Nacional at 10 am.

That left him only 3 hours for sleep. He started to get used to this kind of intense living.

He still had to prepare some papers for this important meeting with the president of ITE's board who at the same time was CEO of the country's largest bank.

He called the doorman and asked for a wake up call at 7.30 am.

When the telephone rang it was only 6 am. It was Mrs. Lappa giving him the news about her husband having been assaulted.

Don Eli looked as one would expect a distinguished elder gentleman to look like. He had sharp cut features, a carefully trimmed "bigote" slim figure of medium height and dressed in a dark gray suit.

He greeted Lic. Guzman and Ernie with warmth and asked Ernie whether he would prefer to speak in his maternal language. When Ernie denied, he showed his appreciation that an American was able to converse in Spanish.

"I have heard that Senor Piper is under the impression that our present public tender is not being handled in a proper way.

Don William could you please outline what irregularities Don Ernesto has found."

Lic. Guzman explained the situation after tender opening, EG having presented the most favorable offer, the continuous efforts by the engineering department to place JB before EG and the tempering with the JB bid documents to be able to justify such action. Guzman did not make a secret of the EG consortium having a person in the engineering department who gave this information to Don Ernesto. The informant simply felt bad seeing the unjust treatment of the first ranking bidder."

"Can you prove these allegations, Lic? Guzman?" asked Don Eli.

"We have a copy of the original JB offer, sealed and initialed as it was received and registered at the tender opening.

The engineering department bases its evaluation on a more favorable JB bid which after tender opening was exchanged against the original bid documents."

"Don Ernesto, what do you want me to do?"

"To relate this information, if necessary supported by the documents Lic. Guzman just mentioned, to your colleagues of the board and please tell them, that any recommendation from the engineering department in favor of JB and consequently an allocation to JB is based on fraud."

"I shall talk to the other members of the Junta, who I think will at least ask the recommending engineer some questions.
How they finally vote is up to them.
As far as I am concerned, I do believe you. It is not the first time that I suspect money was paid to influence decisions.
I trust Lic. Guzman. He has never disappointed me. Since he has presented your case in a convincing way, I shall make it my own cause. But Don Ernesto don't be too optimistic. Of the nine board members only three normally vote with me. The other five directors belong to different political groups and traditionally vote against us."

◆   ◆   ◆

When they left Sala's office Ernie had the impression that this was actually the first time he had somebody's attention and commitment who really mattered.
Don Jepe, the country's president easily could prevent any wrongdoing, but after their meeting Ernie doubted that he would intervene the way he had hoped for.
The decisive board meeting was in four days.
For the afternoon Guzman had a meeting arranged with Don Javier Quiro, the board's vice president, which Ernie would attend just by himself.
Basically Quiro said the same as Elia Sala, that there were two political groups who mostly voted in line with their party. Quiro as an independent businessman and was leaning more towards Sala.

Before the meeting with Javier Quiro he had visited Lappa in the hospital San Juan de Dios where he was bedded in a single room. His wife and son were with him. He looked weak and apparently was suffering from great pains.
Lappa confirmed, what they had assumed, he had been attacked the very moment Jim and Ernie had left his property.
Fortunately there were no serious injuries, no internal blooding, just lots of pain. Apparently the professionals, who had beaten him up, had instructions to just incapacitate him for a few days, so he could not come to the office.

All that done Wim and Ernie had to wait patiently for the board meeting to take place.

◆   ◆   ◆

El Gordo besides being a successful CPA and consultant to some major companies was an associate in a lumber business in the "selvas" of the San Carlos province. They exploited the immense rain forests of the Atlantic lowlands.

He invited Jim and Ernie to spend the weekend with him in the jungle.
Early on Saturday morning he picked both of them up. Still dark they passed in his Land Rover, Costa Rica's most popular four wheel drive, through coffee plantations. Later the morning, coming to the lowlands, they drove alongside endless ranches with Cebu cattle.
Cebus were the only cattle which withstood the hot humid climatic conditions of recently cleared rainforests.
Clearing and settling the rainforests in Central America followed its own rules.
The first to set their foot into the virgin jungle are the lumberjacks.
They enter with earthmoving equipment and open primitive tracks.
These clearings are the start point for the exploration the trees to cut are selected and marked. Only the trees which bring the most money are felled and pulled to the main tracks where they are loaded on trucks and transported to saw mills.
Once the lumberjacks had their first choice settlers move in. The settlers pick the land they want to work, in general only the easy accessible land. The vegetation left by the lumber people is cleared, mostly just set on fire. Within a short time there is an abundance of grass on which robust cattle like cebu feds.
The saw mills usually become the center for urban developments, drawing commerce, churches and schools after them.

El Gordo and his two guests arrived around lunchtime at the wide but calm Sarapiqui river which was the last boundary of civilization.

On the opposite side was El Gordo's section of "selva" where he and his associates had exploitation rights.
A primitive old ferry boat hauled them to the almost untouched land. The only sign of human activity was the track leading into the jungle.

When they reached the other side and left the ferry, their Land Rover was soon stuck in feet deep red mud. A tractor had to pull them up an approximately 30 feet high river bank

Once up it took all of El Gordo's driving skills to keep the car moving. After about three miles they arrived in the lumberjack's camp. It was a cleared space perhaps the size of a football field with a few primitive wood houses, a small workshop and fuel depot.

They stopped in front of one of the houses. A "peon" came to unload their vehicle. The belongings were placed in a big room which would be their common bed room for the next days.

They had a lumberjack's lunch, consisting of generous sizes of boar, hunted by the lumber people, lots of tropical fruit and sour cream.

Everything was paradise-like, except for the mosquitoes. Fortunately El Gordo had brought enough repellant for his guests, foreseeing that they would be the preferred targets of these bloodsuckers.

They passed the afternoon heat, resting in hammocks. After sunset Jim and Ernie went out for an exploration tour.

They carried powerful flashlights and machetes with them. They had been in this kind of environment before, Jim in Asia and Panama, Ernie in Dahomey and Togo in Africa.

They took one of the paths which had been cleared by the lumber people.

The lumberjacks had spotted prints of a jaguar.

There was no need to use the flashlights. The moon was full and shining brightly. They did not want to scare animals away.

When they came close to where the imprints of the Jaguar were found they looked for a place from where they had a good view if the animal should show up.

They sat there for some 30 minutes, listening to the many sounds of insects, birds and the loud roaring of the monkeys. Suddenly they heard or sensed the presence of a larger animal. All at once it became silent. They were excited, their hearts hammered—. hunting fever.

They were tense, all senses alert. It had to be the jaguar; they saw a shadow moving catlike, smooth, and slowly absolutely silent.

Then for fractions of a second, it held in and then in an angle of some forty five degrees took off into the woods.

Jim and Ernie were up in an instant. Forgotten was where they were, what they did and where they went. Running in the direction where the shadow had disappeared. Their eyes had adapted to the darkness. They managed without the flashlight in order not to scare the animal; the moonlight just gave enough light to avoid obstacles.

They probably followed the animal for two or three minutes, right into the thickness of the jungle. Now it was absolutely dark. No more moonlight, even at daytime it had to be dim underneath this dense tropical vegetation.

The jaguar, if it was one, was gone.

Then they became aware how foolish they had acted. How could one run presumably after such a dangerous animal in the dark of the jungle?

They should have known better.

Now it was too late.

They stopped amidst the impassable thick vegetation of huge plants, broken and slippery trees and branches. They were aware, that now during the night they only would make things worse if they moved any further. So they decided to stay right where they were and wait for daylight. Then they would move carefully trying to find where they had got lost.

With their machetes they cleared a little spot where they could more or less comfortably spent the night.

Making the best of it they enjoyed the sounds of the wilderness and a little later they fell into a sound a healthy sleep.

The sun was rising before 5 am and soon they heard El Gordo calling their names. The little adventure came to a quick end and over a hearty lumberjacks breakfast they were the night's heroes and had to take plenty of jokes about the jaguar that probably was only a raccoon.

Arriving back at San Jose, late Monday afternoon a message to call Lic. Guzman was waiting for them.

Guzman had good news. So far four members of the Junta had promised not to support a recommendation in favor of JB. They were only one vote short to bring the JB fraction to fall. Guier was optimistic. One board member who usually voted with them would return shortly before the board meeting from a trip outside the country. He had already been briefed by telephone about the importance to support their fraction.

Jim and Ernie had a small dinner and went to bed early. How good to be back in a nice clean hotel and enjoy the achievements of civilization.

When they met the next morning for breakfast and Fred Morris from JB was facing them from an opposite table, they were aware, today was the day of all or nothing.

Guzman was going to call them as soon as he had any news about the fifth member's commitment for their cause.

They were paged when they had lunch at the hotel's restaurant. It was Guzman.
"I am at the airport to pick up Mr. Sanchez the board member we have been waiting for. He missed his plane in Miami. Whether his next connection, a TACA flight which is due to arrive at 6 pm leaves him enough time to come to the board meeting, I sincerely doubt.
We might have a pat situation.
I am heading now to the ITE board room. Stay in reach, I might need you."

"How long do you expect the meeting to last?" asked Ernie.

"It should not last longer than two hours. I think, I have news and call you before 9.30 pm."

"We keep our fingers crossed, good luck Mr. Guzman."

Two hours later Guzman called Ernie:
"Very bad news, Don Ernesto, Don Eli had a traffic accident. He is hospitalized."

◆   ◆   ◆

Don Eli Sala despite his age of 77 years was a very active man. Besides being president of the ITE board of directors, the Junta Directiva, he was Chairman and CEO of the countries largest bank.
The office from where he supervised and directed both entities was located in the Banco Nacional.

This evening was the board session where the allocation for the San Antonio project would be made. Anticipating that this might become a longer meeting than usual, he had planned to take a little nap at home and have an early dinner with his wife and daughter.

He took the elevator to the ground floor of the Banco Nacional building.
His black Mercedes conducted by a bank employed driver was already waiting for
him. They left the basement and the car was directed to the Salazar residence in
Los Yoses, usually a ten minute drive.

The moment the Mercedes left the bank and entered into the rush hour traffic of
the 1st street, a black Cadillac, waiting in front of the bank was set in motion and
followed Don Eli's slowly driving car.

When they approached the intersection of 1st street and 2nd avenue, the traffic
light being green, the Cadillac behind them for no obvious reason, started to
sound his horn like crazy. Don Eli's driver, Paco, tried to make room for the
recklessly pushing car. He concentrated not to hurt any of the many pedestrians
who had left the narrow sidewalk, waiting for the first chance to cross the street.

The moment Paco entered the 2nd avenue, his light still being green, an old dirt
truck, license plate, driver everything that could be used for identification, hidden behind a thick layer of mud, speeded towards Don Eli's car. People standing
nearby, screamed and jumped aside in panic.
When Paco saw the truck heading towards him it was already too late to avoid
the collision. The truck hit the rear part of the Mercedes, where Don Eli was sitting, with full force.
Fortunately Don Eli was sitting on the opposite side of the impact.

Before anybody could react, the truck pulled back from the badly damaged Mercedes and speeded away from the site of the accident.
Traffic police and an ambulance arrived within a short time. Both Don Eli and
the driver were taken to a nearby hospital.
Apart from some bruises and smaller cutting injuries neither of them was hurt.
Paco was sent home. Don Eli who besides the minor injuries had suffered a shock
was kept in the hospital.

Of course he would not be able to attend tonight's board meeting.

Nobody was able to find out what really had happened. The dirt truck had disappeared; nobody had seen more than a mud covered dirt truck.

So was the black Cadillac who had literally pushed Paco into the dirt truck's path.

◆   ◆   ◆

When Jim and Ernie learned about the accident, they had little doubt that this was another planned action of the group benefiting from their competitors allocation.

They took a taxi to the hospital where Don Eli and Paco were treated.

They wanted to meet Lic. Guzman, to see whether there was any possibility to postpone the board meeting and to find out more details about the accident.

Guzman who only briefly came in, said: "This is all Quarry wants, to preside the meeting. He and the people who support him, would never deliberately give up this advantage.

We have really done everything. There is nothing I can do for you now. I call you as soon as the meting is over."

The two friends went back to the hotel and stayed at the bar. The operator was informed and would page them immediately.

When at 9 pm they still had no news, they called Guzman's home. His wife who answered the phone was wondering too about the unusually long meeting but did not have any news.

They were in no mood to spend more time at the bar. Ernie took a walk to the ITE building to wait there for the meeting to end.

There were some twenty cars parked in front of the building. He walked up and down the street, always keeping an eye on the small exit door where the board members were supposed to come out.

It was almost midnight, when the door opened and the first people came out. They boarded their cars and took off. Guzman responsible for the protocol and formalities was the last one to leave the building.

He was not surprised to find Ernie waiting for him.

"Caldera explained the engineering's department's decision to recommend JB.

Then it came to an argument with Antonio Canvas, a board member who supported the Westinghouse bid, first with Caldera and when it became really ugly, even with Don Andy Quarry, ITE's president.
This took a good while and had not been expected.

When I came forward and objected that the bidder with the most favorable bid was EG, and the two members who were committed to support me, only gave some lame background murmuring, I found myself instantly attacked by both JB supporters and Canvas.

It had never become so obvious that corruption and bribe money was the only thing that mattered for this allocation.

It is a shame that our country has come so far.
I would not be surprised at all, if our highly respected President Don Jeppe also has his hands in this.
How else could he so vigorously deny corruption in state owned and controlled institutions?
He is too smart to be that ignorant and naive."

When they reached the hotel Europa, Guzman stopped to let Ernie out.

Ernie had forgotten to meet Jim at Georges. But he did not have to wait long, when Jim knocked at his door.

They sat together in Ernie's room.
They felt defeated.
They had put all their energy into this; it was almost Easter; since early November Ernie had only lived for this project.

He was exhausted, sick; his stomach hurting probably an ulcer.

Jim not being in a much better condition, felt sorry for his friend Ernie.

PART II

"Lost A Battle—Not A War"

Chapter 1
The Retreat

"Let's make our travel plans, Ernesto,"
Jim was trying his best to end their depressive mood.
"I am glad it's over. In Germany they have a saying: "Better a horrible end, than horror that never ends.""

"Now we know that the only thing that counted were the bribes, for who and how much.
They were never interested in getting a power station at the best price and the best conditions for their country.
They want money for themselves. Let the people or never mind who pay for it.
Under these circumstances we never had a chance."
Our competitor has a network of collaborators who have no scruples.
They are supported by the most influential people of this country.
And within ITE the big guys get the big bribes and the little ones, what can they do? As long as they can at least make a little money on the side. they are better off than fighting their superiors."

"Cheer up Ernesto, take it easy!
We were driven by our own will and by our high ambitions. You fly home and in one week you will be working on another interesting project.

Ernie reflected a while then answered:
What you say is correct, Jim. But when I picked up this project, I knew, it would not be easy. There is no business without complications, sooner or later.
There were some unexpected and unfavorable developments which we had, let me say, still have to face.
We were at a point where we also easily could have won.
The two missing board members would have changed the entire outcome.

Jim have put too much into this, we can not just give up. If you come home with empty hands, your people are going to give you a hard time.

Under no circumstances do I return home and admit defeat. We have to find a way to fight this on a different platform."

They sat there quiet and thought about their situation.

"ITE can allocate this business to JB but they don't have the money to pay JB, unless they get it from the Worldbank. And the Worldbank releases that money only after its approval of both: allocation and contract.

The Worldbank is financing this project entirely at very favorable conditions: grace periods, long term and low interest; a so called soft loan. Costa Rica could do nothing without this Worldbank loan.

Germany is second to the USA the country with the highest contributions into the Worldbank funds.

The countries with the highest contributions are represented by governors. These governors together with the Worldbank's president McNamara set the rules for the institutions policy.

Being such an important contributor the governor for Germany has to be a very influential person. If it came to his knowledge that the bank's funds are used in part, to pay bribes to corrupt Ticaraguan public servants, he would be obliged before any approval, to start an investigation into this tender."

"So Ernesto, what do you want me to do?"

"A little while ago I felt depressed, it was more than one could take. But the fact that this allocation was made only on considerations of bribes, asks literally for a continuation of our fight. Though an allocation normally ends the competition in a tender, here things are far from normal.

I think we still have very good chance winning this business if we handle it in a rational way."

"We had Willy Brandt's support here. Nothing has changed. This is a sovereign state and greed was stronger than his influence.

Things are different with the World bank.

Intervening there, he would not ask for a favor.

He can demand that his taxpayer's money is not used to bribe Ticaraguan functionaries to decide against one of his country's important manufacturers leading to unemployment and misery in Germany."

"Jim, why don't you again call your union friend Graboski?
One of his high ranking contacts should call Germany's governor with the Worldbank. All we want is to present our case to them before they approve this allocation and have they do an investigation into this tender and its allocation procedure."

"Jim you have to call your boss anyhow. I am sure he will appreciate if you tell him how things are and what plans we have to get this business.
If you say it is out and over, he has to admit defeat with all the consequences for the factory and for him.
Since they started manufacturing the turbines trusting that Willy Brandt's intervention would have the result expected by all of us, it is anyhow too late to put things on hold."

Jim agreed that Ernie's way to see and handle this was still the best option for all and then, he had to admit this business was really not lost.
The Worldbank still had the last saying.
As once was said: "It's just a lost battle, not a lost war."

He called Graboski.
"Oh yes everything is fine. Brandt personally sent a telex and we met the president the same day. But the president's intervention came too late; we should have called you earlier.
The last word has the Worldbank; anyhow they give the money for this project. And a good part of this money comes from Germany. Germany has a governor at the Worldbank to who we want to present our case. Can you get us an audience with the governor, as soon as possible?"

"I am glad I could help you last time. I know what happens if you return without that order,—unthinkable!
Don't worry, get some rest. I'll call you back, when it's time for you to get up."

Jim's phone rang a little after 8 am. It was his boss, Hans Nott and Graboski.

His boss started: "Before you give me all details about the situation there, we called Prof. Ehmke. He is helping again. He talked already to Prof. Sohn, secretary in the ministry of economics and in charge of everything related to the

Worldbank. Sohn called me a few minutes ago. He will contact Dr. Stedtfeld, the German governor, as soon as their offices open.

Now Jim tell me what's really going on in Costa Rica."

Jim gave him a detailed report. They had talked for about half an hour, when Nott interrupted: "I have Stedtfeld on the other line, I call you back."

Nott called 10 minutes later.

"I briefly explained to Dr. Stedtfeld that a tender in which we as a German corporation ranked first will be allocated to the third ranking competitor and that we can prove that the documents which led to the allocation had been tampered with.

Stedtfeld proposes to present our case in an official form in a meeting where besides him, Mr. Petersen in charge of Latin America and Mr. Ahmed in charge of Central America will participate. We agreed to have this meeting on Thursday, March 20th, 10 am.

He assured me that everything regarding the San Antonio project is on hold; no approvals or money. Everything is suspended till after our meeting."

Now it was time for Ernie to call his boss. He had not talked to HH since their visit to president Figueres. Naturally HH was expecting more favorable news. Ernie tried to highlight the cooperation of the World bank and ICE being forced to obey the rules of international public tendering.

HH did not buy it.

"That you are still missing a rational judgment, I blame on your inexperience. When Jordan told you that this was a lost cause, you could have given up. You would have saved us a lot of money. You should have heard to an older experienced colleague. I hope this will be the only time you let the company pay for your ill judgments.

What really upsets me is, that even now you are trying to paint this with pink colors. You not only try to talk us but also our partners to further pursue this lost business, to throw their good money after bad money.

You are crazy to involve all kinds of governments, secretaries, heads of states, the World bank for your purposes.

Ernie, you have lost your mind. You have lost and you have to accept it.

Learn from your mistakes. The next time you have to do a better selection. Only take projects where everything is set and arranged that we get the business.

I expect you in the office latest the day after tomorrow."

That was more than Ernie could handle. He was too sensitive to take all this blame. He was anxious to be encouraged and motivated to continue his fight.

HH's reaction was understandable perhaps correct, but for Ernie it was at that particular time, [yesterdays defeat, despite all his efforts to prevail] totally destructive.

He wanted to be alone. He left the hotel, he had to have some fresh air and relax; forget the business and the people he worked for.

It was not worth it. He had to think of himself of his health and well being.

His stomach felt very bad. He could take positive stress almost without limits, work seventy two hours in a row. But destructive negative stress that affected his stomach. He was not cold blooded, cool, set back.

He was hot tempered, vicious, he gave it all, there were no limits.

On his way back to the hotel, he ran into Jim. Jim was alarmed, that his friend Ernesto after the telephone conversation with his boss, obviously irritated, had left the hotel.

Ernie told Jim what had happened.

"We have seen how you handled this difficult job, how you always found ways, I daresay spectacular ways, out of desperate situations when everybody else would have given up. I have talked with Dr. Nott about you. If your people do not appreciate the way you handle this, we would be proud to have you on our team. I will have Dr. Nott call HH about this."

"Let's go to the travel agent now, to rearrange our tickets."

Being close to the Easter holidays, they had problems to find reasonable flights.

Jim finally decided to stick to the reservations he had made before. He would take the previously booked flight and meet his family on Good Friday.

Ernie booked a KLM flight from Panama to New York. From San Jose to Panama he would fly with Copa, a Panamanian carrier.

They went back to the hotel to make some good bye calls to Lappa, Fonseca and their agent.

Ernie would meet Olga for dinner in the Casino Espanol.

Jim and his Costa Rican girlfriend would join them.

A farewell dinner,—would they ever meet again?

◆   ◆   ◆

The morning after the board meeting Don Andy Quarry asked Sigul, Caldera and Nota for a meeting in his office.

"That was much more difficult than we had anticipated." opened Quarry their little conference. "I am glad it's over, I did not expect any objections from Ing. Sanas. Nobody ever told me that he had an interest in Westinghouse."
"Ing. Sanas has visited us on two occasions with an engineer from Westinghouse." commented Caldera. "He never gave reason to assume that he is so belligerently taking the cause for Westinghouse."
"Apart from the few comments Lic. Guzman made nobody even mentioned EG. Good for us that Don Elia was not there. His partisans rely totally on him. Without him they do not dare take a position.
Too bad for him that he had this accident. At his age things like that can easily bring his career to an end."

"Life has become dangerous these days," commented Lic. Nota, "I have lost a good friend in a traffic accident, Lappa was almost pushed over the "Puente los Anonos", then he was beaten up and still is hospitalized; now this hit and run accident with the president of our "Junta". I wonder who will be next."

His words stood in the room giving everybody a moment to reflect whether this was just a comment, or was it an accusation and he was right, who would be next.

Nota was the first to break the silence.
"Should I publish the allocation in "La Gaceta"?"

Everybody was glad Nota had come to the point, the reason of their meeting.
"That is what the law requires." said Caldera.

"Ing. Sigul would you telex JB that they have been allocated and are invited to discuss and sign the contract." Andy Quarry took the word,
"and notify the Worldbank of our decision. But you should do that in person. Same as before, make a presentation in Washington and explain our decision. In that case we are not losing time with their approval. Though it's only a formality, we need their money."

"Assuming that a contract with JB is signed in two weeks, there should not be any problem to deliver and set up the four units before the dry season starts.
I have to detail all this in my report to president Figueres. He also wants a comparative sheet showing the allocated versus EG. As you know the German government has contacted Don Jepe about this tender and he wants to be able to explain our decision."

◆   ◆   ◆

About the same time while this meeting took place in Quarry's office, Ernie boarded the Lacsa flight to Panama. He was wondering whether he would ever come back to this country. Although he had masterminded how to continue their fight with support of the World bank, yesterdays reprimand by his boss had left profound traces. His self-confidence was at the lowest point since the time of his adolescence.

He was disappointed. Being that close to success, all his dreams would have been fulfilled and then this end.
In Panama he had to wait three hours for the departure of the KLM plane. He killed the time with some cans of Panamanian beer.
The plane came from Peru. It was a DC 8 Super Long. A delegation from Eastern Germany, the communist part of Germany, was on board. He tried to catch what they were talking about. Impossible—they were used to communicating with voices so low that somebody not belonging with them would not understand a word.
Finally the time for boarding had come. the plane was not full. The seat between Ernie and a man from the East German delegation was not taken.
When they were airborne, Ernie tried to start a conversation with his neighbor from behind the "iron curtain". He learned that he and his comrades were returning from an official visit to communist Chile (Allende's regime) and Peru.

They had been flying for approximately 30 minutes, the flight attendants had just started the bar service, when all in a sudden except for the emergency lights, all lights went off.
The bar service was immediately stopped and after a little while an announcement was made:

"Ladies and gentlemen, this is your captain. I regret having to inform you, that we have a failure in our electric system. There is nothing to be concerned about. We shall land at the closest airport which is the island of Trinidad."
Some 10 minutes later the lights of an airport became visible.
They circled a few times around the airport, then ascended and left the airport behind them. Everybody was alarmed.
Ernie's neighbor form behind the "iron curtain" finally said something:
"They are getting rid of the kerosene, they refueled in Panama. I am sure we will return to the airport we just saw."

Exactly as predicted by his fellow passenger, after some twenty minutes they again approached the airport.
They were flying low.
Fire engines with lights flashing framed the runway.
They made a 180 degree turn and approached for landing.
Everybody was ordered to bend down and protect their heads with seat cushions.
The absolute silence and the ghostlike emergency illumination added to the tension everybody felt.
The flashing lights came closer and closer. The runway was just in front of them. They approach very slowly, now they were over the runway, the engines went dead; they touched ground—very softly.
They felt safe, relieved. It was over.

Mobile stairways were rushed to the exits of this extremely long aircraft.
The DC 8 Super Long because of its length had a reputation of having bad service, too few toilets and being unsafe in cases of emergency.
They were led to the terminal, from where after a few hours they were transported to nearby hotels.
They were supposed to wait for a replacement plane which was flown in from Amsterdam.
The hotels were not prepared to feed so many unexpected guests. So the food, marinated fish (ceviche) from Peru was brought from the plane.

Ernie who had no food since the early morning ate what was offered. He went to his room, took a shower and was glad when, after another long stressful day he finally got some rest.
He could not have slept long, when troubled by a strong pain in his stomach he woke up. The pain became worse and worse. He felt an irresistible urge to vomit.

He hardly made it to the bathroom. He could not stop vomiting. There was blood. Weakness overwhelmed him, he fainted. Time passed. He had lost any feeling for time. He was still laying on the bathroom floor. The slightest movement and he vomited again, blood. His head was bursting with pain.
He would never leave this room again. He stayed there on the floor waiting for his end.

After a while the urge to vomit ceased. He was able to slightly move, and after some time he was able to crawl to his bed.

He fell asleep. When he woke up it was bright daylight.
He felt better, much better. The pain in his stomach was gone. so was the urgent nausea.
A little headache, extremely shaky in his legs, the hands trembling but hungry.
That was close. Never in his life had he felt so close to death even with a desire to die just to end the suffering.
He went to the breakfast room and had a bowl with porridge and drank almost a gallon of water.
After that he felt almost as good as ever.

The plane from Amsterdam came around noon.
Ernie arrived at JFK, New York late afternoon.
He changed to a Mohawk flight to Albany.
From there he took a rental car and when he finally opened the door of his apartment in Schenectady it was almost at mid night.

Although it had been a long travel day, he had fully recuperated and looked forward to talk to HH.

Before 8 am he was in the office. This was the best time for some serious words.
HH was already there and gave him a friendly hello.
Ernie's reaction was cool.
"When you gave me this job you knew that I am an easy to motivate person. You knew I would be committed entirely to whatever project I decided to take up.
That is what I did with this Costa Rica project.
Bringing the consortium together, making the best offer, fighting for support up to the countries president and the Worldbank.
The commitment, energy and ideas I put into this business deserve merit.

Instead you have blamed me for wasting the company's money for a lost cause, which I already at the very beginning should have identified as such.
This was unjust and destructive.
As easy as you can motivate me, just as easy you can destroy me."

"Ernie I am sorry. I did not want to hurt you. Your commitment is highly appreciated. The way you were involving and even manipulating even high ranking politicians is uncommon.
If you prove that your way is successful, I shall learn from you."

"Dr. Nott has called me from Germany and asked me to let you join him at his visit to the World bank. Although I am convinced that this business is lost, I respect your and his judgment. He wants you to meet him on March 17th in New York. You have my blessing. I am anxious to see what comes out of all this. And again no bad feelings, I am sorry."

Ernie went to his desk and checked the mail which had come during his absence.
There were two public tender which he caught his interest.
One was the electrification of 84 communities in rural Colombia. A turn key job: diesel power stations with substations and transformers.
Financing had also to be offered.
The other one was very similar to the San Antonio project in Costa Rica. Four gas turbines for the Orinoco region in Venezuela. No financing.
He picked the gas turbines for Venezuela. With Manis he had already a motivated partner. He called his friend Otto Nunz in Essen, Germany.
First they had a long chat about the business they both had started, in Costa Rica.
"We at Manis really enjoy working with you Ernie. I heard that HH is giving you a hard time. I know that Nott would do almost anything to have you in his team. Working together in Venezuela, that's a great idea. We have our own office in Caracas. They can help us much better than the two ladies in Costa Rica.
But anyhow we should get Juliano Maldecara on our side. He is the best. With his support and the same concept as in Costa Rica, a consortium, we will beat everybody."

When Otto hung up, Ernie thought about Otto's idea, work with Maldecara as their agent.
"If you can not beat him—make him your ally."

Contacting Maldecara for Venezuela might even open new perspectives for Costa Rica. It certainly was worth thinking about it.

Ernie made a copies of the Petroven (the client in Venezuela), specifications and put them in the mail for Otto.

Chapter 2
The World Bank—A Powerful Ally

Ernie took the Easter holidays to prepare documentation for his discourse at the Worldbank.

Nott's flight from Germany was scheduled for Tuesday afternoon. Ernie spent the morning in the office and took an early afternoon flight from Albany to meet Nott at JFK in New York.

Nott, led by three gentlemen—one obviously an immigration official—was the first Lufthansa passenger to come out.

"So you are the one who keeps the governments busy on both sides of the Atlantic." he greeted Ernie.

The two gentlemen who were with Nott were Mr. Goldstein, the Manis lawyer in New York and Mr. Rosenstock the shipping agent.

Mr. Rosenstock's S-class Mercedes, most recent model, was waiting right in front of the terminal. They went over the Queen's bridge to the Plaza hotel at Central Park.

Nott and Ernie were led to their rooms and met a little later at the Oyster bar, a popular New York hang out and meeting place.

They had some delicious Blue Point oysters, some dry white wine, and lots of small talk and a heated discussion about wines: which one, what year, temperature, to what food and other trivialities.

After a while they went to the Oak Room, the formal restaurant in this prestigious hotel. Mr. Goldstein, apparently a frequent guest, in the hotel's premises had made a reservation for their party of four.

Nott and the two New Yorkers, originally Jews immigrated from Germany, were great lovers of gourmet food and expensive wines.

For Ernie it was an enjoyable experience. A glimpse into the lifestyles of the rich and "beautiful".

Rosenstock's driver was supposed to pick them up early next morning and drive them to La Guardia airport, from where the shuttle to Washington leaves.
The first available shuttle was at 10 am, leaving more than enough time for their meeting with Dr Stedtfeld, which was at 2 pm.

Dr. Stedtfeld was a tall slender man in his mid fifties. Gray seemed to be his favorite color. He was dressed in a gray suit, had gray hair, gray eyes, gray shoes, gray tie. He greeted them formally but friendly. His secretary offered coffee and cookies. They had some small talk, speaking German. After a few minutes the secretary opened the door for two gentlemen. Now the language changed to English. Stedtfeld made the introduction. The two gentlemen were, Mr. Petersen, in charge of the Latin America division and Mr. Ahmed referent for Central America.
Then Stedtfeld gave the word to Ernie who explained what had happened from the moment of bid opening when they were ranked first to the decision of the "junta" to allocate JB.
He highlighted that this decision was based on tampered with bid documents and that he was in possession of a photo copy of the original bid documents. He also mentioned that they had alerted president Figueres who simply ignored their allegations and refused to take any action.
"These are severe accusations," was Mr. Petersen's first reaction.
"If this can be proved, Costa Rica will have a political scandal."

The phone was ringing, Stedtfeld; picked it up and briefly talked to somebody.
"That was Robert McNamara; he wants me to see him in his office. If you would excuse me, I will be right back."

Being alone with Petersen and Ahmed, Ahmed asked Ernie:
"You don't have the copy of the original JB offer with you, do you?"

"No I left all documents with my colleague in Costa Rica."

"Mr. Sigul from Costa Rica was here two days ago. He left the bids of the top ranking bidders here. If I had your copies, things could be sped up."

In this moment Stedtfeld returned.

"I mentioned your case to Mr. McNamara. He wants somebody as soon as possible in Costa Rica, to do an investigation which should not be limited to this case but also the entire credit situation. If corruption on these levels is confirmed, there won't be any future credits to this country.

Payments to Costa Rica are on hold till we have the results from the audit."

Petersen briefed Stedtfeld about the conversation they had during his absence. Ernie would fly immediately to Central America to bring the documents required by Mr. Ahmed.

The meeting was concluded, very much to Nott's and Ernie's satisfaction.

They went to Ahmed's office to answer some technical questions.

Neither Nott nor Ernie could give him the information required.

Golden would accompany Ernie to assist him with his technical queries.

◆   ◆   ◆

Two days earlier, when Sigul left the Worldbank he had the feeling that his relationship to Mr. Ahmed for some unknown reason had changed.

Sigul, head of ITE's engineering department was Costa Rica's principal contact to this important financial source.

He had expected to return to his country with the Worldbank's approval of their allocation to JB.

It was the first time that he left Washington with the decisions pending and uncertain. When he tried to push for an approval, Ahmed responded in a rather cool and arrogant way:

"Don't be so pushy Mr. Sigul. The bank has to verify that all requirements have been met and that the allocated bidder really is the best choice. The Worldbank dislikes any pressure to force preferential approvals."

Without their approval it would be premature to invite JB for contract negotiations.

The day after his return he met with Caldera and Nota in Andy Quarry's office. Everybody had taken the banks approval as a formality. When Sigul explained that the bank had rebuffed him when he insisted in the approval and that therefore they could not even discuss a contract with JB. Only then his audience began to understand the consequences for the project's time schedule.

JB would not start manufacturing without a contract and the initial payments.

"Don't you think it's possible that one of JB's competitors, probably EG has presented their case to the Worldbank?" asked Quarry.

"To be frank Don Andy, I had the same idea. If that is the case, the way they are fighting for their business, we can expect some serious problems."

After the meeting Caldera phoned Maldecara.
"Fernando good you called me. I heard from Levy that you made some deals together.
I have nothing to do with that.
Only now I have learned, how Levy, who was supposed to get the original JB bid, got these documents and that the same documents are momentarily on their way to the Worldbank.
Levy messed up everything; we do not work with him anymore. He is out.
So anything you do with him, it's your business. But watch out—he can cause problems."

"I could not reach you Juliano. I had to do something. At some point EG had the majority of the board members.
The reason I am calling Juliano, the first payment is due."

"Your allocation is not worth a penny without the World bank's approval. From where do you think, Fernando, you get your money?"

Caldera knew he was in trouble. He had a deal with Levy, he had used him twice. He owed him $ 10,000. The payment was supposed to be made the day after the allocation. Levy had called a few times.
His last call was an open threat:
"The money was due more than a week ago. If I have not received the $ 10,000 by Friday, you get a reminder you won't forget."

He had to pay Levy tomorrow.
There was no way to get the money from Maldecara that quick.
He would have to advance the sum out of his pocket. His family was wealthy. His brother or one of his cousins would help him out, and then there was his aunt, late president Caldera's widow.

◆   ◆   ◆

Dr. Nott and Ernie took the shuttle back to New York. At the hotel they were met by two gentlemen from General Electric who had arranged a dinner in one of New York's most "in" restaurants.

They saw some well known faces; otherwise it was a crowded and loud place with average food at astronomical prices.

The next morning after breakfast they said good bye, Nott had an afternoon flight to Germany. Ernie was leaving right away for his flight to Costa Rica.

Jim was at the airport in Costa Rica to pick him up.

They exchanged news. Lappa was back in the office and looked forward to talk to Ernie.

Jim was glad to get out of Costa Rica and make the trip to Washington.

The news Ernie brought from his visit to the Worldbank, made them feel good. This had been another uncommon initiative which seemed to produce positive results.

"It was depressing to stay here alone. I have become used to discussing things with you and always finding a favorable solution."

"I felt pretty much the same." said Ernie, "We have become a good team.

◆   ◆   ◆

About the same time Caldera arrived in front of what had been his beautiful home, his and his wife's pride.

Fire-fighters were all around, fighting the flaring flames which were consuming all his belongings rapidly.

On his way home from the office he had already seen the blaze in the early night sky long before entering the exclusive Nunciatura neighborhood.

Levy's threat: "a reminder you won't forget", gave him an early sensation, that something was wrong at his home.

His heart hammered. He tried to accelerate his car.

The rush hour traffic, fire engines, police cars everybody seemed to head in his direction.

He went to the officer commanding the fire fighters and introduced himself.

Everything was like a dream, unreal, the heat, the noise of burning dry wood—like gunfire, the blaze of the flames.

He stumbled: "I am the owner, is somebody inside? Is my wife somewhere? Where is our servant? We have a dog, is he still in the house?"

"There seems to be nobody in the house. A young girl, probably your servant was in shock, she has been taken to a hospital."

She insisted that nobody was in the house. Your wife is visiting some friends in Los Pinares. We have tried to reach you at your office, but you had already left."

"Do you have any idea what happened?" asked Caldera.

"It is still premature to say anything. Together with the police and the OIJ we will do an investigation. There are many possibilities: a short circuit or your maid was incautiously handling something that caught fire. Even arson is a possibility. We will see."

At this moment Caldera saw his wife's car coming. She opened the car door, was blinded—one outcry—he ran to her.

◆　　　◆　　　◆

It had been much more difficult than he thought.

Nobody gave him the $ 10,000 he so desperately needed. He had asked his brothers, his aunt—negative.

The worst was he could not tell them what he needed the money for. Too often he had come to borrow money and always he had been slow in paying his debts.

Typical for Ticos he often spent more than he had.

He called Levy and asked him to wait till Monday. Levy just hang up, without saying a single word.

Well he had dealt with the mob, these were the consequences.

But that was not the end. He was no coward, not the man to let Levy, a foreigner, a gringo get away with this.

Levy would pay, there were ways.

◆   ◆   ◆

Jim and Ernie went to Georges. Much to their surprise Olga was not there. She had sold he place to a guy from Panama. He stood now with his girlfriend behind the bar and did the job Olga had done before.

Ernie called Olga's home. The maid answered and told him that Olga was getting trained as a flight attendant for Lacsa in New Orleans.
Ernie was glad for Olga. A job like that was much better for her than running the bar.

Ernie called Lappa's home. They agreed to meet next morning at the hotel. It was Saturday.

Lappa had news.
"Caldera's house burnt down. They do not exclude arson. The papers are filled with photos. There are many rumors.
It's a week since I am back to the office.
Although I am excluded from almost all meetings, it's an open secret, that there are problems with the Worldbank. They say that the JB allocation has not been approved and payments are suspended."

"That is correct, "answered Jim, "we are just coming from Washington. At this point we can not give you more details.
Let your people know, if they have problems, we are still interested.

If we get the business with your help, there will be a little compensation for your sufferings."

"We are flying home on Monday," said Ernie,"if you have any news give us a call."

They accompanied Lappa to the parking lot. The flow of information would not cease. This was Lappa's only chance to benefit from this business.

◆   ◆   ◆

Fernando Caldera had a sleepless night at his aunt's home. He had no doubt that Levy was behind al this. His house was insured. He would not suffer any financial loss. The insurance company there was only one, was state owned. The president of INS, that was the abbreviation, was a good friend of his.

Levy had no idea with who he had messed up.

Caldera's mother was the sister of one of the most popular and powerful presidents. Many of the country's top positions were held by his family.

The highest ranking officer of the OIJ, the Costa Rican FBI, was his cousin. They had a very intimate and confidential relationship. He would brief his cousin about Levy, former CIA and Mossad agent always armed and responsible for many crimes in and outside Costa Rica.

They knew how to deal with people like that.

The next morning his cousin Rafael woke him up. He showed him "La Nacion" the daily newspaper. There was extensive coverage with photos of his burning home.

"Cousin Paco just called. He wants to talk to you, the OIJ is involved.

That went much better than Fernando had anticipated.

He called Paco the man in charge of OIJ and asked him to meet at their aunt's home.

They had breakfast together. Fernando gave his cousin Paco all necessary background information about Levy. He was being blackmailed. Levy had some compromising knowledge that had to do with his job at ITE.

Not giving in, Levy had first threatened him and then set his house on fire.

"We know this guy. He is extremely dangerous. He is a professional killer; he used to work for the CIA and the Israeli Mossad. Now he is on Somoza's payroll. We have been after him for a while but were never able to prove anything.

We will deal with him. He won't bother you anymore."

◆   ◆   ◆

David Levy felt safe. In this country of "cabrones", there was need for people like him. His services had been used by highest ranking politicians. They protected him. People like Fernando Caldera were little fish, "pendejos".
If they did not comply, they had to learn the hard way; they had to be kept in fear. This he owed to his reputation.
Caldera would find a way to pay him the $10,000.

It was past noon. He was still in bed.
A woman in her mid twenties, long legs, well shaped buttocks, firm breast, immaculate skin an insatiable black eyed tropical beauty made him want to stay were he was for the rest of his life.

He did not realize how close he was to the fulfillment of this wish.

With lazy movements the female body crawled on top of him.
Soft sensual lips, an experienced slowly probing tongue and demanding hot flesh touching seductively his vulnerable parts.

Those were the pleasures he was deeply enjoying when the door of his bedroom burst open.

From being lost in the most gratifying actions of sex to desperately fighting for his life it was only an instant.
Levy had his heavy semi automatic Colt instantly in his hand and was aiming at the intruders.

He did not have the slightest chance. Before he was able to bend his index finger, the OIJ officials had ended his life.

The man who had caused so much suffering and pain to so many people had passed from the life's greatest pleasures to death in fractions of a second.
What a pleasant way of dying.
The girl, who had lead him from paradise to hell, was unharmed.

Paco Caldera who had personally led the operation called his cousin Fernando and reported:

"Mission accomplished."

"Levy tried to shoot at us and was killed in self defense."

◆   ◆   ◆

Before 6 am the next morning Jim and Ernie checked out of the hotel Europa which had become their second home and went to El Coco airport in Jim's rental car.

A Pan Am flight took them to Miami where they changed to an Eastern Airlines flight to Washington DC.

They took a cab to the Washington Hilton.

It was a beautiful early spring day in March.

The sun was shining. The nicely arranged flowerbeds, the flourishing trees loaded with red, pink and lilac blossoms reminded one of a spa and health resort in Europe.

Ernie called Mr. Ahmed at the Worldbank and set an appointment for 9 am the next day.

Since they had no particular plans they took a sightseeing tour to all the well known attractions of the nation's capital.

On the way back to the hotel they ran into the Itachi sales manager for the USA, Joshi Tanaka. Since Itachi was one of the consortium's partners they agreed to meet for dinner and talk about their common business in Costa Rica.

They met at a nice sushi restaurant not far from the Hilton hotel.

A friendly Japanese hostess traditionally dressed took care of them.

"So JB is giving you a hard time," Joshi started the conversation.

"They are desperate for orders. They have not sold a single unit the last six month."

"According to GE they are closing a deal over fifteen units in Saudi Arabia." commented Ernie.

"That's what they would have liked to happen. Itachi got that allocation yesterday. JB is out. They played all their trumps. Being British still means a lot in the Arabic world.
But with their union problems they could not commit to a firm commissioning date and their prices were by far too high."
So the Saudis went Japanese."

Ernie and Jim reported about the Costa Rica business.

"I don't know whether your intervention with the Worldbank was such a good idea. I have heard through our sources that JB had the British ambassador talk to Mr. Petersen, the man in charge of Latin America.

As you well know the British diplomats are much more aggressive than their German counterparts.
You might have a chance with the delivery time. JB has union problems and same as in Saudi Arabia will not make any firm commitment."

Wim and Ernie were a little disillusioned. A lot of what Yoshi had said made sense.

"This Costa Rica business is extremely difficult. That is the reason we only participated as "silent partners".
If you are against Juliano Maldecara and if you have no agent with superb connections you are fighting a very difficult battle."

The next morning Jim and Ernie still were under the impression of Tanaka's comments the night before. He might be right but for them it had been better to nourish from their naivety. They did not feel too good going into the meeting with Ahmed.

Ahmed gave them a friendly welcome and was very pleased with the help Wim was able to give. Both went through the technical specifications of the bids submitted by Ing. Sigul.
Then Ernie handed him the copy of the original technical bid specifications which Ahmed carefully compared with the ones Sigul had given him.

"This is unbelievable. This is fraud. Under normal circumstances the loan agreement would be cancelled. I have talked to Mr. Petersen and Dr. Stedtfeld about this possibility in case your allegations would materialize.
The further procedure has to be stipulated on a higher level."

Ernie and Jim had done everything they could think of.
Their mission with the Worldbank was completed.

Jim would go back to Central America and watch the further development and Ernie would return to his office in Schenectady.

Chapter 3
Uncertainty

When Jim arrived back in Costa Rica, he found a message from their friend Fonseca. Fonseca was asking him to return his call as soon as possible.

Since it was already past 11 pm Jim decided to call him the next morning.

Tulio Cesar Nota, ITE's lawyer and Fonseca's friend suggested a dinner at Fonseca's house. Jim agreed to meet Nota the same evening at "El Gordo's" home.
Jim was wondering what Nota had in mind.
Nota had been on their side, in the critical moment, however, he had changed fronts and worked against them.
As long as he was careful, only releasing information which he wanted their opponents to know this might be an opportunity. But Jim was well aware that was a slippery snake—he had to be alert.

"El Gordo" picked him up at the hotel. They made a stop at a fish market, bought fresh fish and shrimp and arrived at the Fonseca residence half an hour before the time set for dinner.
Jim declined when he was offered a drink. He wanted to be completely in control of himself and would stick to water and coffee.

Nota arrived a bit later than the agreed time. He seemed a little embarrassed. The only time Jim and he had met, was the night of Lin's fatal accident in front of the hospital.
Through his friend Fonseca he had let Jim know, that the only reason he had changed fronts, was to get the money offered by Caldera to compensate Lin's family for the loss of their son.

He tried to be friendly: "Jim you like Costa Rica. You have been here only two month. Your Spanish is excellent. You have a diligent female professor."

"You are flattering me, Don Julio, I need many more lessons."

Everybody was laughing—the ice was broken.

"You live the life of a playboy. Taking the best here and when you are bored you travel two or three days to Miami to enjoy the gringas."

Jim understood. Nota knew, he had been out of the country. He certainly suspected that Jim had part in the activities at the Worldbank which were directed against them.

"I am in charge not only for this area. We have also projects in the US and in South America."

"There are rumors that people from your company have visited the Worldbank."

"Don Tulio, the company I am working for employs more than 300 000 people. A company of this size and importance to the German economy always has close contacts to the Worldbank."

"Now we are playing cat and mouse. You know that our Ing. Sigul was in Washington notifying the World bank of the allocation of the San Antonio project. Why should I deny that he encountered difficulties? You probably know more about this matter than Ing. Sigul himself."

Jim had immediately seen his chance to use Nota to launch a horror scenario at their opponents. This scare tactic could get ITE to come up with its own initiative to prevent a cancellation of the Worldbank loan.

"Don Tulio, it is no secret that there are problems with the allocation of this tender and the Worldbank is far from approving it.
You should be prepared that the Worldbank will conduct an investigation of the entire tender procedure and an audit of all documents.
Depending on their findings the loan agreement can be cancelled and your country can be blacklisted for loans from development banks.

Because of these severe consequences for the entire country the implications for everybody involved in the wrongful allocation from the highest ranking politicians to ITE's functionaries can well be imagined and anticipated."

Nota took the bait.
"All this would not benefit you.
If there is no money there is no business.
Golden listen well, if ITE signs a contract with you, would you honor the services which lead to this?"

Jim had to hold back, not show his triumph.
It was out.
ITE, was looking for options.
That was the reason Nota wanted to meet him.

"Don Tulio, we are always prepared to honor services rendered to us. But please do not misinterpret this. Our prices only permit the payment for services; we have not made other provisions. I hope you understand what I mean."

The next morning Nota met with Caldera in Sigul's office. He reported of his meeting with Jim.

"Golden from EG came alone. Piper is back in the US. Though he did not confirm any personal visit to the Worldbank he admitted that they are in close contact with this institution.
Golden seems to be very confident that the bank will deny approval of the allocation to JB.
He gave me to understand that they are prepared to pay for services but have no provisions for major as we would get from JB."

"There is no need for that. JB has already started manufacturing of the turbines. With that delivery time is no issue anymore," commented Caldera.

"We should sign a contract with JB as soon as possible. Once we have a contract I can take it to the Worldbank and press for approval," said Sigul.

"If JB accepts penalty on late delivery, the legal part is ready for signing," said Nota.

"The technical part is also ready," added Caldera.

"Well, then lets inform the media, TV and newspapers, that the signing of the contract will take place this Friday," concluded Sigul their meeting.

◆   ◆   ◆

When Ernie arrived at the office, he could not resist the impression that sarcastic remarks were made about the way he stuck to his Costa Rica business.
He felt hurt, that after all his effort he had become a victim of mockery. HH did not make any comment, he almost ignored Ernie.
It would be the best to put this project aside. He had done everything. If his judgment was right, then things would develop their own dynamics and time was working for him.
He concentrated on the Venezuela project and worked in close cooperation with Otto Nunz from Manis. Within the next weeks he would meet Otto in Germany to put the final touch on their common offer.

After he had been back for about a week, HH called him into his office.
"Ernie I am glad you came back to your daily routine work and you are not wasting more time with this banana republic business. Dr. Nott just called. They also gave up this business. Golden left Costa Rica yesterday. Poor Golden is down and disillusioned. JB signed the contract Friday last week.
Nott was furious. He called Petersen at the Worldbank. Petersen who apparently feels pressure from the British ambassador told him that it is not the Worldbank's business to promote suppliers. If there was an investigation, which he did not want to confirm, the results would be given to Dr. Stedtfeld, the German ambassador.

Ernie was slightly shocked. He had firmly trusted that he was on the right track, never mind what the others said, now he could not fight the impression that he had something missed.

HH saw his reaction.
"Cheer up, Ernie, this is over. You will do great with other projects.
Put your energy into this Petroven business in Venezuela. That's worth it.

I never had a good feeling about this banana country. These greasers are no partners for reputable US companies. That is where the Europeans have an
edge;—they simply bribe their way into business and are even allowed to deduct
these contributions from their taxes.
Blame it on our discriminatory legislation."

Ernie had to admit that HH was right.
It was against the law, to "smoothe" the outcome of public tenders. This was
active corruption, a crime.
Their competitors in Europe and Asia had no law which prevented them from
bribing functionaries in third countries in order to get a business.
They could never match competitors like JB with an agile agent like Maldecara
who was simply buying favors and contracts for his European masters.

The next two weeks he dedicated exclusively to the Petroven tender. His trip to
Essen in Germany had been approved by HH. He would fly in four days and
planned to stay there till end of next week. That should be enough time to bring
the two parts, EG and Manis together and finally have one common offer.
He would do everything to avoid mistakes which were made in Central America.
The more he thought, the more it became obvious to him, that he was getting
lost again in pure paperwork. This was the time when all efforts should be made
to promote and secure this business directly with the customer.
Same as happened with ITE in Costa Rica, Petroven would make decisions with
who to contract long before tender opening.

He desperately needed somebody to personally and professionally arrange things
now with Petroven.
The bid opening ceremony was a formal act, not more.
If he waited as he had done in Costa Rica, he had learned nothing.

Then he had an idea—perhaps a crazy one....

◆   ◆   ◆

After Jim's meeting with Nota, Jim felt disgusted by Nota's and his colleagues'
greed.

The only interest of these public functionaries was to take advantage of this government project which was supposed to help the Ticos (Ticaraguan people) and was paid by taxpayers from other countries.

History had shown that this country would never pay these loans back. One moratorium would be negotiated after the other.

The Ticos always had excuses and they would always find somebody or something to blame: falling coffee or banana prices, earthquakes, volcano eruptions, excessive rainfall or droughts—just disgusting!

Dishonest corrupt functionaries like these, their egoism, insatiable appetite for money and luxury, their political ambitions as well as ignorant politicians like the country's president, were to blame that their country would never progress.

But Jim also felt good.

These functionaries who openly supported JB had approached him. It showed that JB was in trouble and that he and his friend Ernie were on the right track.

If they only continued to put their opponents under pressure, they would succeed.

When Jim returned to the hotel, he found a message from Lappa. Lappa wanted him to stop by on his way home.

Lappa had news which was in total contradiction to Nota's approach.

ITE had agreed with JB to sign the contract the coming Friday.

Lappa had prepared a press release, describing the San Antonio gas turbine power plant, its purpose, financing and how lucky the country was to have the Scottish JB company to execute this important infrastructure project. It was briefly mentioned that JB a Scottish company had been favored ranking first before competitors from all over the world.

President Figueres would attend the signing ceremony and give a speech. Everything would be extensively covered by the media.

Jim was perplexed. Nota and his JB supporting friends had moved quickly. Since the EG consortium had not agreed to step in for JB and assuming the JB payments for bribes, the corrupt functionaries pushed the signing to make this a "fait accompli".

Jim wished Ernie was there. They were the perfect team. Together they might find a way even out of a desperate situation like this.

He called Dr. Nott to give him the bad news. It was only 2 am in Germany when he woke his boss.

It took Nott a while to get his brain working. When he finally captured what was happening, he suggested a call to Petersen at the World bank and press for the promised investigation.

If the Worldbank announced this investigation before Friday, the signing would be off.

That was the reason behind this rush to sign the contract. ITE was concerned that the Worldbank could announce such an investigation any time and so putting everything on hold.

The next day when Jim had his lunch at the hotel's restaurant, he was paged, it was his boss.

"Oh Jim it is all over. Petersen refuses to do anything that could favor us. It is not his job to promote suppliers. I should not call him any more, it might be contra productive.

I tried to get hold of Stedtfeld; he was not in the office.

I have the impression that the British governor is intervening on JB's behalf.

Jim no more time, no more money for this damned Banana country. Arrange your return flight and come home.

I will call HH and tell him that it's all over."

Jim booked his return flight to Germany with a stop over in Venezuela to check the situation of the Petroven project, Otto and Ernie were working on.

◆   ◆   ◆

Lappa's press release appeared as important news at the bottom of the front page of "La Nacion" newspaper.

Starting at 9 am Friday morning the ITE assembly hall began filling. A crew from the national TV network was already there. they put their equipment in place and talked to ITE personnel trying to get some additional information. Reporters from the only newspapers La Nacion and La Republica had also arrived and talked to Cargas and Lappa. The JB people, Fred Morris and the company's lawyer, entered together with Sigul and Caldera.

Andy Quarry, ITE's president, Juarez Tejido, ITE's General Manager and Jose Figueres, President of Costa Rica solemnly entered the hall at 10 am.

Cameras flashed and the TV crew became busy. Everybody rose and some invisible sound equipment played the national anthem. Suarez Mejido went to the speaker's desk and held a short speech. He welcomed the country's president and briefly talked about the importance of the project.

Andy Quarry followed him. He said about the same and added: I am very proud that this project will be executed by a company from Scotland, the land of my ancestors. I wish my late father who immigrated to this country in the year 1929, could be here to welcome the old shipbuilder JB in his new homeland."

President Figueres gave a political speech highlighting his achievements and how good the country would be off; when in two years he passed the presidency to his successor.

The TV crew tried to get all of the president's and the highlights of his predecessors' discourses on their cameras. The press people took lots of photos and were busy scribbling whatever was said.

Then the actual signing ceremony took place. Licenciado Nota with his pastoral voice started reading paragraph after paragraph of the contract.

Then the contract was passed to president Figueres who signed first, then the two JB people followed by Andy Quarry, Juarez Tejido and finally Lic. Nota sealed and initialed everything.

The act of signing had become an unusually great event. Normally the contract would only have been signed by ITE's general manager and the authorized JB delegate.

It was obvious, the ITE functionaries by making this such a public event they wanted to make it irrevocable. Declaring a contract like this null and void would make the president loose his face before the entire nation.

Jim watching everything on TV experienced a similar crisis as Ernie a few weeks before when he was ordered home.

But gaining back his temper and analyzing what was happening one had to admit that this was only a tremendous show pulled by some scared and corrupt public servants who feared that an investigation would unmask their fraudulent manipulations and they would end up loosing.

If the Worldbank did not pay, the Ticos could make all kind of speeches and celebrations, San Antonio would either be built by the EG consortium or not built at all.

The pressure on the ITE functionaries was on, more than ever.

The evidence in the hands of the Worldbank had been recognized by Ahmed and could not be neglected.

An investigation into ITE's allocation procedure and an audit was simply a logical consequence.

The pompous signing had not changed anything for the consortium; their prospects were better than they had ever been.

But there were difficult and embarrassing times ahead for ITE's functionaries and for Costa Rica's president Figueres.

◆   ◆   ◆

About two weeks after this "final defeat" Ernie had an unusual idea.

He picked up the telephone and called the international operator to give him a telephone number in Rio de Janeiro.

"Juliano Maldecara that is all I have."

The operator called Brazil talked briefly to the operator there and, Ernie almost could not believe his luck, came up with Maldecara's phone number in Rio.

Ernie hesitated shortly, he was excited. He made himself clear what he was about to do.

If he dialed that number he would have his opponent on the other side.

The individual whose ideas and actions had more influenced his mind and his life the past five month than anything else.

But this was also the person who JB owed everything and whose connections would also decide the outcome of the Petroven business.

On the other end of the line was the key for success in Venezuela and who knows.... .Ernie had never given up the Costa Rica business.

He was desperate for some feed back from their opponent about the situation in Central America from their opponent's perspective.

After Petersen's brushing off Dr Nott and his warning not to call again, there was no contact with the Worldbank. Nobody knew whether an investigation had already begun.

Ernie firmly believed that their intervention with the Worldbank would pay out, just a matter of time and patience.
But patience that was one of Ernie's weakest points.

So what..... .

He dialed the number. Somebody picked up the phone:"Hello!"

"Can I speak to Mr. Juliano Maldecara?"

"Speaking!"

Although only two words had been said, the very strong New York accent was evident.

"Mr. Maldecara, I am Ernie Piper your opponent in the Costa Rica business."

"I know you. What do you want?"

"Mr. Maldecara we have been fighting each other for some time now. There is no end in sight. This is to no ones benefit. We are both wasting our resources. I think it is time to sit together and talk and save our time and money for more rewarding projects.
Although the contract for this business has been signed, we know about ITE's and JB's problems and that the last word on this has not yet been spoken."
Maldecara did not argue and was listening. Ernie continued.
"We are working on other projects where cooperation between us might be good for both."

"I am always open for a good proposal."

Now Ernie was caught. He had overstepped his competences. The best simply to admit it.

"Mr. Maldecara let me call you back within the next hour with a firm proposal for a meeting."

Ernie was overwhelmed. He had made contact with his main opponent. It had been so easy—unbelievable. Just calling the international operator, another call and the man who had so much influenced the last months had become a human, somebody he could talk to. He was exited.
That's why he liked his job. Nothing was predictable, total personal commitment, hard brainwork, ups and downs but also moments like this.
He felt great, he was back in business.
What to do next?
His boss, HH was on a business trip and difficult to contact. He had promised to call back with a proposal in one hour. Nobody in EG Schenectady was adequate for this kind of negotiations with Maldecara.
This weekend Ernie would fly to Essen, Germany. The best would be to have Maldecara come to Essen.
He picked up the telephone and called Nott.

"Dr. Nott you won't believe what I am telling you ..." he told Nott the story in all details.

"Ernie, you did great. I always wanted to talk to Maldecara. Invite him to our plant in Essen. We make good power stations, have good prices, but we have bad agents. Maldecara could be an excellent fit. We need some time to discuss this in all details before he arrives. Tell him Tuesday or Wednesday next week would be very convenient for us."

Ernie called Maldecara before the hour was over.
"Our partner Manis in Germany would like to invite you to discuss cooperation in Latin America. Would next Tuesday or Wednesday suit you?"

"Fine with me. I will arrive next Wednesday in Duesseldorf. My partner and assistant Ernst Sommer as well as my wife and son come with me. Please arrange pick up at the airport and hotel reservation. I am going to telex you the flight number and arrival time."

A little pause, then he added much to Ernie's surprise:
"By the way Mr. Piper, you might not know yet, you did a magnificent job in Central America."

This comment coming from Maldecara filled Ernie with joy. But what did Maldecara know. Had the Worldbank investigation taken place, did he know the results?
With the signing of the contract all contacts, even Lappa, had gone over to JB. He had left numerous messages for Lappa and Fonseca to call back—no response.

Ernie would not have been Ernie if he had left it at that. Something had happened in Costa Rica. It could only come from the Worldbank. He had to find through Ahmed with who he had a relatively good relationship.

Calling Ahmed's office, one of his colleagues told him that Ahmed was not available.

◆   ◆   ◆

The same day only minutes before Ernie had made his first call to Brazil, Maldecara received a call from his contact person in the Latin America department of the Worldbank.
"Ahmed has left this morning for Central America. There will be an investigation. There were sufficient signs of irregularities to justify such an action. Be prepared for any kind of trouble."

When Maldecara shortly after this heard Ernie's voice, he instantly thought of a coordinated action. This hyperactive youngster who never accepted defeat and always came up with a new surprise had become his nightmare.
All his experience of thirty years dealing with governments told him that dark clouds were forming on the horizon.
For these underdeveloped countries the Worldbank meant everything.
The Ticos had no choice; they would not hesitate to accept any decision or recommendation made by the institution.
He could not remember one case where a competitor called for the bank's intervention.

But this was certainly a hell of an effective move by his opponents which even after a contract had been signed would turn everything to their favor.

What an embarrassment for the Ticos who had insisted in that pompous signing ceremony.

Since he was the one to know better than anybody else on what fragile ground the contract with JB was formed, he did not give it any chances to survive an audit.

They all would look for him as a scapegoat.

With JB he would loose his most important client.

Costa Rica would declare him persona non grata.

The invitation to Manis in Essen, Germany came like a gift from heaven. Manis was one of the main players in the gas turbine business thanks to Dr. Nott they were very motivated and easy to deal with.

Not like the Brits, the Germans had no union and labor problems and their prices were good and not like the Americans they were open to include "NA's", an abbreviation for "Nuetzliche Abgaben", commissions which helped to get the business.

They would make an excellent fit.

And last not least he looked forward to work with this "jack in the box"-guy Ernie Piper who seemed to operate on his wavelength.

He called his associate Ernst Sommer and briefed him about the new developments in Central America and with their opponent in Germany.

"When you are done with the booking, give me all available information about the Petroven project in Venezuela. I think that will be the first business we work together."

After Sommer had left his room, he called Petroven in Caracas. He asked for Mr. Sanchez, head of the engineering division of the largest Venezuelan corporation, owned by the state.

He said a friendly hello to his longtime friend, with who he had done numerous gas turbine compressor stations.

When he asked Sanchez whether he was already committed, Sanchez replied: "Make me an offer Juliano, and then we shall see. You know I like to work with you Juliano."

Chapter 4
The Investigation

Maldecara's information was correct.

The Worldbank had sent its regional referent, Abdul Ahmed to San Jose, Costa Rica. Ahmed carried a letter from Mr. Petersen directed to ITE's president with him.

In this letter the president of ITE is asked to give Ahmed access to all documentation and files related to the evaluation and allocation of the San Antonio project. ITE's president is requested to make sure that Ahmed receives full support when requesting verbal or written information.

The letter points out that severe allegations of fraud and manipulations to favor one particular bidder had been made and that irregularities found in the bid documents submitted by Mr. Sigul supported these charges.

For situations like this an investigation is a procedure stipulated in the agreements between Worldbank its member states.

On his flight to San Jose, Ahmed met a colleague from the BID, the Banco Interamericano de Desarrollo, an institution operating similar to the Worldbank, focusing, however, on the development of the American countries.

Since both entered the country together, both showing their diplomat passports and also went together to the hotel Europa the rumor went out that they were two Worldbank inspectors.

Ahmed called Andy Quarry's office and asked for an urgent meeting.

Entering Quarry's office formally greeting and presenting the official note, Quarry knew that this visit meant trouble.

Nevertheless when his eyes went over the letter, it was more than he could take. He changed from pale to red to pale and when he finally tried to make some comments a non understandable stumbling came from his trembling lips.

After a while regaining control he called Sigul into his office. In Ahmed's presence, without showing the note to Sigul, he ordered Sigul to personally assist Mr. Ahmed and give him any information and document demanded.

He complimented Ahmed and Sigul out of his office.
Alone in his office he tried to analyze the situation he just had been confronted with.
He had exposed himself for a company just for being Scottish, fighting for JB at the board session. With his remarks about Scottish heritage and pride in front of the media he had ridiculed himself.
He had acted like an old sentimental fool.
Although he personally had nothing to do with the subject of the Worldbank's allegation, as president he was responsible and he had to admit, that he to willingly had accepted Caldera's proposal to allocate JB.
To be honest, he had always suspected that his engineers had given "money motivated" recommendations.

The Worldbank's note was an insult for ITE the institution he headed, and the entire country.
He had to call president Figueres, to admit that he had failed and that he would take the blame for the disgrace caused to the country.
Too important was this matter. A suspension of loans from the World bank and other development banks such as BID due to fraud and corruption would be fatal for any government. The consequences could be devastating for fragile systems like theirs.

But top priority was to talk to Caldera and Sigul alone. He regretted having ordered Sigul to assist Ahmed without previous discussion with his two most involved subordinates
"I am not in control of things anymore. My own people have probably already taken advantage of my trust or to be honest of my weaknesses."

He picked up the phone and called Sigul: "I want you and Caldera in my office, immediately!"
He did not have to wait.
"Mr. Ahmed is investigating whether both of you are corrupt."
He made a little pause.
"This is the official note from the Worldbank—a disgrace for ITE and Ticarauga.

Read it, Caldera—loud!"

"If the allegations are true and the investigation leads to this conclusion, you will face severe consequences; I will see to that, you can be sure. You are dismissed.

Then he called president Figueres;
"Don Jepe we have a problem.
The Worldbank has suspended the loan for San Antonio and has sent its referent who in this very moment is starting an investigation and audit about the allocation of this tender to JB.
Since issues of this delicacy can be harmful for our country, I feel it is my duty to inform you."

"This is very generous of you Don Andy," the president's ironic undertone could not be overheard, "I want you in my office tomorrow morning, 7 am. You did not expect this brief information on the phone is all I am entitled to. I want all details. Come prepared."

Don Andy Quarry was no young man. He was in his mid sixties. He liked his job. But today had been too much for him.
He felt tired, old. Why not retire and enjoy what remained of his life. He had a large finca at the Arenal volcano where they soon would build a hydro electric power station and flood the valley to create an artificial lake.
He would probably use the meeting with the president to give him his resignation.

◆   ◆   ◆

Earlier this afternoon, when Sigul accompanied Ahmed into the engineering department, he tried to re-establish the good relationship they always had. In previous occasions when Ahmed came to Costa Rica, Sigul took him out for dinner or even invited him to his home.

"Mr. Sigul, my mission is to investigate irregularities supposedly committed in your department. I am sorry, but my job obliges me to a strict neutral and independent relationship."

"Mr. Sigul, I want to get this over with as quick as possible. What I need is a room, where I can work undisturbed. I also need a telephone with an outside line and access to a secretary.

I would appreciate if you could introduce me to your coworkers and all people working in your department. If anybody has travel plans, I would like to know now in order to arrange my interrogation schedule accordingly.

I will try to do my job with as little interference in your work as possible."

Sigul showed Ahmed his department and introduced him to his subordinates. He asked Caldera in his office.

"Mr. Ahmed needs an office and a telephone with a direct line. Would you please move into Lappa's and Cargas' office?

When I introduced our staff to Mr. Ahmed, I asked everybody to give him their support. When I am here, I personally will see that Mr. Ahmed needs are met. In my absence will you take care of Mr. Ahmed? Needless to say where and what our interests are."

Ahmed moved immediately in Caldera's office. He asked Sigul for all evaluation records, including personal notes and the original offers of all bidders who had participated in the San Antonio tender. Files were rushed into his office and simply piled on the floor.

Without wasting a minute he started the audit.

Ahmed had done this investigative job before. He knew, although everybody was assuring him of their cooperation, they would try to find ways to hide every evidence that could be linked to manipulations of the evaluation.

Fortunately he had already studied the top ranking bids which Sigul had brought to Washington and compared with the incriminating documents submitted by Golden and Piper.

He would now try to find notes and evidence on which the tampered with JB bid was based on.

And he hoped that his interrogations would reveal how, when and who exactly had tampered with the bid documents.

If high ranking officers, e.g. ITE's president or high ranking politicians e.g. the country's president were behind this, it was likely that the loan agreement would be cancelled definitely and the country was not eligible anymore for loans from international development banks.

If the tampering had been done on department level it was more likely that ITE would be allowed to correct the allocation without further implications.

An eventual legal prosecution of the individuals responsible for these actions was in the hands of the local authorities. The findings of his investigations could not be used for criminal prosecution.

Ahmed anticipated a two week job. Once he better knew the people working in the engineering department, he would ask somebody to assist him.

He strongly hoped there would be some time left to explore the attractive Ticaraguan countryside.

Ahmed went over the first lot of files and notes piled all over the place and sorted out what would be studied first. He had a key to the office. When he left late that evening for his hotel, he locked the door. He was sure there were more keys and it was likely that someone would enter to check what he was doing. He positioned a sheet of paper in a way that somebody entering had to move it. At least he would know when somebody spied on him.

◆   ◆   ◆

Before leaving the office Quarry asked Sigul to assist him to prepare for next day's meeting with president Figueres.

In front of him was Caldera's recommendation for the junta to allocate the project to JB.
"If I go by these documents and the comparative evaluation JB's bid is the best. So please help me, what does the Worldbank know that I don't know."

It was obvious that Sigul was embarrassed.
Since Ahmed's arrival he had anticipated this interrogation by his boss and the subsequent interrogation of his superior by the country's president.

For Quarry everything looked as if it was in order. That had been the purpose of manipulating the JB's bid,—their recommendation had to look genuine and was not supposed be questioned.

"There is a possibility that JB abused our trust and somehow was able to tamper with the original bid. It could be that the Worldbank got hold of the original bid and the documents which I submitted for approval were tampered with.

Andy Quarry, did not expect from a subordinate who, as things looked, was disloyal and corrupt, to admit his wrongdoing.

He felt disgusted.
"The way I know you Sigul, this means the allegations are correct and the data I have in front of me, are not the ones of JB's original bid.
You want to save yours and Caldera's neck.
Do not think you will be let off that easy. There are too many important people involved.
How do we, how does the country look in the eyes of the Worldbank and foreign governments.
If the Worldbank's allegations are confirmed, the contract with JB is null and void; JB and their agent will be declared "persona non grata" and will be no more permitted into our country.

Tomorrow's meeting with president Figueres will decide what steps will be taken against our own functionaries involved in this scandal.

For my meeting with president Figueres to morrow morning, I want a written report signed by you and Caldera within the next 30 minutes.
I wait for it.

◆   ◆   ◆

After having read the report Andy Quarry had handed him, President Figueres was furious with his longtime partisan Andy.
His German visitors had been right.
ITE's policy and decisions were influenced by corruption and a president who showed more loyalty to a country his father had immigrated from than for Costa Rica.

"You and your subordinates pushed a bidder who by no means was in the best interest for our country.
You put your own interests before the interests of the institution you are heading and before the interest of our country."

Figueres made a little pause to let his accusation settle.

"Andy I am deeply disappointed about your disloyalty.
Once we fought side by side and you were prepared to give your life for our just cause.
I gave you one of the most attractive jobs this country has to offer.
I was so naive to trust and defend the organization led by you. You talked me into signing the contract with your supplier.
I look like an old fool and the opposition will jump on this."

"I should ask you to give me your resignation and have your engineers prosecuted. The uproar this would cause would make things even worse.
For the time being nothing will change. We have to wait what the investigation unveils. Then we will act.
Stay in contact with the best bidder, that's the EG consortium if I am not wrong. Make sure that they can immediately take over and do the job, the moment JB is kicked out.
Do everything to keep the loan agreement with the Worldbank alive.
The country is in desperate need of this additional source of electric power. The San Antonio plant has to be built and to generate power before March next year. I would never forgive you, if because of this affair we loose access to Worldbank loans or if the construction of the plant is delayed.

And I want the personal files of everybody who is involved in this disgraceful affair.
This will have consequences."

Quarry was embarrassed and felt ashamed.
Not only had the president hurt him with his reference to the old days and their close friendship, the way he showed him how to do his job were prove of his deficiencies as president of the state owned utility company.
The way the president had taken him on, did not even leave him a chance to give him his resignation as he had planned.

He would do that once he had taken care of everything president Figueres expected him to do.

He felt so exhausted and tired and just looked forward to a peaceful and stress free life on his finca in Arenal.

◆   ◆   ◆

It was Sunday afternoon, when Ernie boarded a Lufthansa 707 to Cologne/Bonn airport in Germany. The plane was almost empty. He had an entire seat row of three to himself.

Taking advantage of so much space, he raised the armrests and made himself comfortable. After dinner he tried to find some sleep.

The next morning when he arrived at his destination he felt relatively fit. Otto Kunz was expecting him at the exit gate. They went to Otto's car a nice Opel, the popular GM car manufactured in its German subsidiary. It was Monday morning rush hour traffic and they had to cross the entire Rhein Ruhr area, one of the most densely populated areas in Europe. Almost eighteen million live in this heartland of Germany's iron and steel industry.

Although they used the Autobahn, the famous German high speed highway, the bumper to bumper, sometimes at breathtaking speed, took them more than 90 minutes for just fifty miles from Cologne to Essen.

Otto gave his friend a tour through the engineering department and introduced him to his colleagues. Then they went with Dr. Nott for lunch.

"Ernie deserves the best food and wine that Germany has to offer." was Nott's friendly welcome.

Unlike to the US, a business lunch in Europe is a major event. Nott's driver was waiting in a black Mercedes in front of the office building.

They went to an expensive looking restaurant in a nearby small town.

During the five course lunch with plenty wine and after dinner drinks they discussed Ernie's conversation with Maldecara and his forthcoming visit.

"So Maldecara mentioned that we still have a chance in Costa Rica?"

Nott started with what was most troubling him.

"He said we did a good job, but did not want to say why," answered Ernie, "I later called Fonseca in San Jose, and to find out if anything had happened. He had heard from his friend Nota that two inspectors from the Worldbank had arrived. This was more like a rumor, nothing specific."

"Then I called the Worldbank and asked for Ahmed. 'He is not available' was the only information I was able to get."

◆   ◆   ◆

In the meantime Abdul Ahmed was making good progress with his job.

During their visit in Washington Piper and Golden had told him that the original of their copied documents was in Lic. Nota's possession.
So the first thing before starting to review the staples of documents piled up in his office, he went to Nota and asked him for all tender and bid documents which for a good reason had not been brought to his office.
With these original documents, all pages were sealed and initialed; it was easy to find the pages which had been exchanged after bid opening.

Having the original offers of all bidders, he made his comparative evaluation. In Francisco Cargas he found a trustworthy person.
After he had Sigul's permission for Cargas to assist him, everything went smoothly.
Cargas was a quiet man, an electrical engineer in his early fifties. He was loyal towards the company he worked for and did not talk about his colleagues or superiors. Ahmed liked this attitude.
Cargas explained how he and Lappa had done their evaluation and what the general criteria for the evaluation were.
It was still necessary to interview Caldera and Nota since neither Cargas nor Lappa had been involved in their work.

Ahmed's evaluation, strictly applying the criteria set for this tender, put the EG consortium first, followed by Nuovo Pignone, Italy and Westinghouse, USA. Considering that JB had not accepted a penalty for late delivery, JB was only ranking seventh.
Ahmed still had to get some additional information for his report. After consulting with his boss, Petersen, he intended to submit this report to ITE's president Quarry and to the country's president Figueres.
For this and possible discussions he estimated another week.

◆   ◆   ◆

During his stay in San Jose Ahmed avoided contact with locals. He had declined invitations from Sigul and Caldera. Once he took Cargas out for lunch.

The evenings he spent with his colleague from the Interamerican Development Bank (BID), his travel companion who he had met on the flight to San Jose. They had the same hobbies; both were amateur botanists and collectors of orchids. Both enjoyed playing chess and liked good food. The few gourmet places San Jose had to offer were soon discovered and frequented almost every evening.

The BID functionary was American but born and raised in the Panama Canal Zone. Live in the tropics and particular in neighboring Costa Rica was familiar to him.

He had finished his job in Costa Rica and was planning to pay his parents a short visit in Panama, before returning to Washington.

He had agreed to accompany his friend Abdul Ahmed on a day tour to one of the close by rainforests. As the weather forecast called for thunderstorms and heavy rainfalls they decided to hike to the crater of the Barva volcano.

The Barva was close and looked familiar since they could see this volcano looking out of the windows of their hotel rooms.

If the weather became too bad, they always would be able to return to their hotel. From the hotel it looked like a 30 minute walk, from where they planned to leave their rental car parked, to the top where the crater was clearly visible.

The dense cloud forest which covered the upper third was untouched virgin territory, except for a marked path leading to the crater. That part of the mountain was their actual goal.

With the rental car they would drive to the limits of the rainforest. From there they planned to follow a trail to the top of the volcano, where a beautiful lagoon and the inactive crater were hidden in the lush untouched "selva virgin".

They had talked to various people who had made this tour recently and according to them, staying on the path, there was no danger to get lost.

Crater and lagoon could only be accessed from the south west, the Pacific side. The cloud forest was part of the widely unexplored jungle territory which reached from Colombia to Mexico and covered the Atlantic and mountain regions of Panama, Costa Rica, Nicaragua, Honduras, Guatemala and Southern Mexico. There was an almost as abundant variety of species as in the Amazon basin.

The day set for the hike was Saturday. On Friday they rented a Land Rover, the most suitable vehicle for the kind of terrain they had to drive.

They bought some films and a plastic bottle to carry drinking water.

Saturday morning after a good breakfast they took the road to Heredia and from there an unpaved way to San Joaquin, a small village.

The villagers were wondering about the gringos driving by and taking route towards the virgin forests of the volcano.

For some time they would be the last humans who saw Ahmed and Weller alive.

They were able to use their four-wheel-drive vehicle for another half hour. Then the way became so bad, that they decided to leave the car and continue hiking. They followed the trail made by ox carts and cattle till they reached a point when they entered the dusk of the cloud forest. The path was now narrow and made by humans. No cattle could pass here. Sun and sky were not visible through the dense vegetation.

It was already noon when they entered the forest—much later than anticipated. If they wanted to make it to the lagoon they had to walk faster. They had to reach the lagoon not later than 2 pm. A short rest and then return. If there was no rain, the return would be easier but they had to rush since they had to be back by the car by 5 pm. At 5.30 it would be night.

The first part of their hike led through rain forest. Vegetation was lush, huge ferns, philodendrons, orchids. Once in a while the sun was still penetrating the almost closed dome formed by high tropical trees.

The deeper they entered the forest and the higher they came, the cooler it became. They must have reached about 8,000 feet. I became foggy, humidity was extreme. Everything was covered with moss of a light gray color. It almost looked like "winter wonderland", unreal, with a little fantasy one could imagine all kind of creatures from fairy tales.

But there were none, no animals, not even insects, absolute silence.

They were now in the cloud forest. Other than the rainforest this type of tropical mountain forest is most of the time in clouds.

No sun, just fog, clouds, extreme humidity chilly—no place to stay long

Marching fast, they reached the lagoon at 1.30 pm.

They were impressed.

The emerald green and totally calm lagoon. Much bigger than they had thought. Since the vegetation was too dense and trees blocking the view it was not possible to see the limits.

The sun was shining, there were beautiful butterflies and colibris and orchids everywhere.

There were thousands of small orchids, species unknown to them. To get to the most desirable ones they had to climb trees which sometimes took them away from the trail.

They had made good some time on the way up; they would be able to descent in even less time. This was a unique opportunity. They never would get a chance like this again to collect species this rare. They moved further and further away from the lagoon and the trail they had used on the way up.

They became careless and did not pay any attention to the fog which little by little had become almost impenetrable. When they finally had problems to spot each other—it was too late.

They could not see the lagoon nor did they know in which direction it was. They stopped and sat down.

It was dusk, the fog so dense they could not walk without bumping on trees or stumbling over roots and rocks. It was not even 3 pm.

Too dangerous to walk, too chilly to sit down and wait for the fog or clouds to pass.

The humidity was penetrating to their bones. They did not carry any protective gear for these conditions. It was supposed to be a day hike in the warmth of the tropics.

They sat on a trunk covered with moss, relatively comfortable but for the chill and the fog which had become a slight rain sizzle and felt worse than frost.

They waited for the fog to clear and waited but instead of clearing it became dark; the night in the tropics comes very fast.

They had to stay over night, they had no choice.

Hopefully the clouds would be pushed down by the early morning sun or just move away, pushed by some breeze.

Every morning they had seen the volcano in bright sunlight from their hotel.

The imminent problem was the cold. It was not even 6 pm, what could they do the next 11 hours before the night was over. They were wet to their bones and the chill made them shiver.

They sat back to back, trying to warm each other. They became hungry; breakfast had been their last food. Weller had some jelly bars, guayaba, half a dozen. They split one and kept the others, who knows what would happen.

It was too cold to find sleep. After a while they rose and just moved to fight the cold. The night seemed to last for ever. At 5 am the dark made room for the same dense fog as the day before.

They were caught amidst clouds.

Cold, hunger and thirst was troubling more and more.
Something had to be done. They could not stay here and wait for miracles. Both had little experience how to survive in this kind of environment. It was not their first time in a tropical rainforest, but that was entirely different to this blinding fog and the chilling humidity.

They argued a long time about the location of the lagoon. If they had left the Pacific side and were on the Atlantic side of the volcano, they were in a different clime zone. In that case they very well could be stuck in fog, clouds and rain for weeks.
Since nobody would ever find them in the endless jungles of the Atlantic they had to make it back to the other side of the volcano, at all cost.

But if they were still on the Pacific side and the bad weather was only temporary, they had to move with caution. If they could not make it back on their own, sooner or later search troops would find them.

They decided to first follow Weller's instinct. They left marks every two meters and followed the direction which Weller deemed correct for one hour. From the point where they started that was not more than half a mile. It was very time consuming to leave marks and to walk cautiously in this dense fog and difficult terrain.
Since they did not find anything familiar they decided to return and walk one hour in the opposite direction. The return was fast in less than twenty minutes.
Then they started in the opposite direction. After only ten minutes Weller shouted: "Abdul, here is a trail, look!"

No doubt, Weller had found a trail. But it looked different than the trail they had taken when they hiked up to the lagoon. It was wider but apparently had not been used for some time. They decided to follow the trail in the ascending direction supposing at some point to hit the lagoon which had to be somewhere uphill.

They marched for two hours without seeing any trace of the lagoon or the trail they had come up. The trail was blocked by fallen trees. They mastered the obstruction and suddenly heard the loud noise of a waterfall. If there was a waterfall they had to be far below the top of the mountain and far below the lagoon which was at the top of the mountain. Either they had it almost made back on a different way or they were on the Atlantic side far from the top of the volcano.

They decided not to take any more chances and to stay here till the fog cleared. At least they had water and they also would find something eatable, berries, fruits or palm hearts.

The vegetation had changed. Almost gone was the moss, there were huge ferns and plants with leaves like umbrellas, "paraguas de los pobres" as the Ticos said.

The fog had lost some of its density and the cold humidity which so much had bothered them last night, was gone.

All they needed was the sun.

If they could see the sun in the early morning they were on the Atlantic side and they probably had to take the same way back.

If they could see the sun in the afternoon they were on the Pacific side and should continue their way till they reached one of the "pueblos" or "fincas"

However, any further step in the wrong direction might bring them deeper and deeper into the Atlantic rainforest where there was no way out and nobody would be able to ever find them.

Never had they so much missed the sun.

The day went by and the late afternoon the fog had descended and was worse than before. They must have been caught in the low pressure system the weather report had forecast.

The early night came and soaking wet as they were, they were shivering of cold. They took again their back to back positions and tried to find some sleep. They ate their last jelly bars. Tomorrow they had to find something eatable.

Whom had they told about their hike to the Barva. Ahmed had briefly mentioned it to Cargas. The receptionist and the bellboy in the hotel Europa had given them directions.

The car rental company also knew about their plan to drive to the limits of the Barva cloud forest. They would miss their car which was supposed to be returned on Sunday.

Petersen would wait for Ahmed's call on Monday morning and would probably call ITE.

Tomorrow was Monday. Only tomorrow one would start to miss them.

The search might start tomorrow Monday, more likely on Tuesday. It did not make any sense to start such a search in the afternoon.

◆   ◆   ◆

Saturday: San Jose, less than 20 miles away, nobody was missing them

Sunday: Same situation; The receptionist had the weekend off, so had the bell-boy. Cargas was not supposed to have any contact with Ahmed over the week-end.

Monday: The room maid was wondering that Ahmed's and Weller's bed was untouched for the second night. She knew that both were friends and called the receptionist.
She had already missed the usual morning chat with Ahmed.
Weller was supposed to have checked out on Sunday.
Cargas was wondering that Ahmed did not show up at the ITE office.
He waited till 10 am before he called the hotel Europa asking for Ahmed.
The car rental company called the hotel and asked for Weller and Ahmed and was concerned about the whereabouts of the rental car.

The receptionist informed the hotel manager that the two guests were missing but also that they had planned to hike the Barva volcano. The manager called immediately the US embassy and the OIJ, suggesting a search in the area of the volcano.

Petersen who was used to call Ahmed around lunchtime at the hotel learned that Ahmed was missing. Since Ahmed was leading an investigation involving the country's highest ranking functionaries and politicians, he immediately thought of a crime. Petersen called the US embassy and explained his concerns. He asked for immediate help.

By Monday afternoon a group of fifty Guardia Civil officials was dispatched to the Barva.
The first sign that they were on the right track: They found the rental vehicle, untouched were the two friends had left it.

They took the same way, the two hobby botanists had taken two days ago. With the appropriate gear they made it to the lagoon before dark.

They set up tents, made a warming fire and enjoyed a night away from home. There was nothing they could do that same day.
They would start their search very early the next morning.

The national TV was extensively covering in its evening news the story of the two missing Worldbank functionaries. Everybody took Weller for a second World-bank investigator.
Other incidents were mentioned where people hiking on the Barva, had become victims of crimes others had disappeared and were never found.

Then the TV anchor came to the point which for the next weeks would keep all media busy and which certainly send a chill into the homes of some people:
"We have learned that the two Americans are Worldbank functionaries who are investigating irregularities and possible corruption of the San Antonio project. The signing of this important project by president Figueres and other dignitaries has been extensively covered only a few weeks ago.
Neither ITE's president nor anybody from the "casa presidencial" was available to comment whether the sudden disappearance of these important functionaries had anything to do with their investigation."

◆   ◆   ◆

It was Tuesday morning.
Everybody was speculating about the whereabouts of the two investigators. After the evening news, the public hungry for sensations, was more than ready to believe, that corrupt ITE functionaries were behind all this.
And the functionaries involved, Nora, Caldera, Sigul and Andy Quarry were meeting and discussing the more than embarrassing situation they were in.
They very much would have liked to be in our two friend's shoes—away from the public and media, hidden somewhere, where nobody would find them, in the cloud forests of the Barva.

◆　　◆　　◆

The two castaways, object of all the uproar had just passed their third night in this ever lasting fog.

The night before they had heard shots which had been fired not too far away from where they were. They shouted as loud as they could but most likely had not been not heard.

They had little doubt that the shots were meant to be signals for them.

They decided not change their location and wait for more and hopefully closer signals. Staying on the trail they had the best chances to be found or once the fog cleared move more freely trying to close up with the search troop.

It was Tuesday late morning when the fog all in a sudden cleared.

There were even spots where the sun was able to penetrate through the dense roof of enormous leaves and gigantic ferns.

All in a sudden everything looked so paradise like so beautiful. Red and yellow blossoms became visible. The greenish grey had turned to beautiful tropical colors.

For the first time they became aware that they were not the only creatures, that there was an abundant bird life. They heard and saw parrots, humming birds and other exotic birds they had never seen before.

They were overwhelmed by all this sudden beauty. For a moment they had forgotten hunger fatigue and their soaking wet clothes.

It became warm, sticking hot and insects, mainly mosquitoes started bothering.

Then they heard human voices which came from not too far away.

They counted and shouted: one, two three "A u x i l i o".

They did that again and again. The voices came closer and closer and then they saw uniformed men of the Guardia Civil.

They had been found they were save—after four days and three nights in the Central American "selva virgin".

◆　　◆　　◆

After being taken good care of in a hospital and answering to all the questions the media had they finally returned to their hotel.

After a good night's sleep and a huge breakfast Weller was able to return the same day to Washington, skipping the planned visit to his parents in Panama.
Ahmed who immediately after their rescue had briefed his boss Petersen about the happy end of their jungle excursion was meeting with ITE's president.

"Mr. Quarry I appreciate your and your staff's cooperation.
I will take this afternoon's flight to Miami and Washington.
Once my report is ready, you will be contacted by the bank.
I am sorry for the inconvenience I caused trying to discover the natural beauties of your wonderful country."

"Can we count on the first payment which as stipulated in our loan agreement is due after signing the contract?" asked Quarry.

"The contract you signed with JB has not been approved by the bank.
There will be no payment without the bank approval."

Andy Quarry tried one more time:
"JB is already manufacturing the rotors for the turbines. They will stop production if they don't get their first 10% payment."

"Mr. Quarry, this is a sovereign country free to make payments and to sign contracts as it pleases.
Our institution's approval of contracts and payments is strictly ruled by agreements with its member countries."

Quarry was sensitive enough to leave it at that.
The question was:
Would the bank simply annul the loan agreement?
Or would it disapprove the allocation and subsequent contract with JB, but permitting another bidder who qualified.

He could not wait for the official report. Once that report was released everything was final.

He would send Sigul to Washington with a proposal, a proposal which would satisfy everybody.

Chapter 5
Meeting with the Opponent

Juliano Maldecara, his wife, his 15 year old son and his associate Ernst Sommer arrived in Düsseldorf/Germany with a Lufthansa flight from New York.

Maldecara coming all the way from Rio de Janeiro had met his family and his associate on the stop over in New York.

Comfort and service for the few passengers flying first class in the relatively small Boeing 707 had been excellent.

When they stepped on German soil they were relaxed and in best spirits.

Immigration and customs formalities were simple and quick.

They were welcomed by Ernie and Otto who carried a Manis sign for easy identification.

"So you are Ernie the guy who spotted me in Rio. I have heard a lot about you, I was looking forward to meet you."

"Well the pleasure is mine Mr. Maldecara. You are the grey eminence in the gas turbine business. Nobody who has not heard about your fantastic successes," was Ernie's polite but honest answer while they were walking to Dr. Nott's Mercedes.

They went in two cars. Maldecara and his wife were together with Ernie in Dr. Nott's chauffeur driven car.

The Maldecaras were true cosmopolitan people. They had been in Germany before and knew all European countries spoke fluently French, Spanish and Portuguese. Their home in Europe was in Estoril, the exclusive beach outside of Lisbon in Portugal.

Maldecara and Ernie liked each other from the first moment they met.

Ernie about twenty years younger reminded Maldecara of his early years in business. Maldecara was for Ernie the incorporation of a perfect business—and salesman.

The driver pointed at tourist attractions and gave explanations in German. Ernie translated for the Maldecaras who showed much interest in everything.

"You are an amazing young man. You speak so many languages and are at home in so many countries." commented Mrs. Maldecara.

Ernie felt flattered. It was nice to meet people who appreciated his way of life.

They went to the Arosi hotel, a medium size hotel, the best Essen a city of almost one million people had to offer. Ernie was also hosted there.

Dinner was scheduled for 8 pm at the famous Schloss Baldenei restaurant an old castle with beautiful gardens.

Before they went to the restaurant they met with Dr. Nott at the hotel's bar. Ernie made the introduction.

Dinner at the restaurant, being one of Germany's best, was an experience by itself almost worth the trip over the Atlantic.

It was a nice evening in late spring. The gardens were beautifully set and everything was blossoming. Later the romantic illumination invited them to sit outside and have some drinks while enjoying their conversations.

"Juliano has high esteem for you, Ernie," said his namesake Ernst Sommer, "The way you handled the San Antonio project, your aggressiveness and persistence have impressed him.

What he most liked is, that you, the young man had the idea and style to call him in Rio and made him, your opponent a proposal to work together. I am sure Juliano will be of much help for your future operations especially in Latin America."

When they left Schloss Baldenei it was already 11 pm, for the American guests that was 5 am New York time. Mrs. Maldecara and son fell asleep on the way to the hotel Arosi.

Juliano Maldecara asked Ernie to join him for a drink at the hotel bar.

"Young man, I know what you think and what you are after. Let me anticipate one thing, do not expect me to do anything or tell you anything that would affect my loyalty towards JB.

You have caused us and are still causing us lots of problems. Let's leave it at that."

They ordered a last drink had some chat about EG, HH and Ernie's personal plans and then went to their rooms.

The next day Maldecara and Sommer negotiated a cooperation agreement with Dr. Nott.
The first project the newly formed alliance would work together, were the Petroven compressor stations in Venezuela. Maldecara had a look at the Petroven offer which was almost finished and made his recommendations.
He planned to travel directly to Venezuela and meet with Golden.
Ernie was going to join them a few days before tender opening, bringing the bid documents with him.

◆   ◆   ◆

Quarry, Sigul, Caldera and Nota were in Quarry's office.
Quarry had called the meeting immediately after Ahmed had left him.
They had a vivid discussion what to do to prevent the Worldbank from cancelling the loan agreement.

"Ahmed's audit will only confirm the bank's allegations. Either the bank uses this to cancel the agreement or they are open for a practical solution.
Why don't we give it a shot and propose a solution that everybody can live with." suggested Sigul.

"That's exactly what I had in mind.
We have to come up with something before Ahmed submits his report," agreed Quarry.
"Parallel to Ahmed's audit we did our own investigation which confirms the bank's allegations.
JB tampered without our knowledge with its bid and was able to improve their ranking so we had to recommend them for allocation.
Discarding JB, whose original offer would have them placed only third, the best bid is the one from the EG consortium who we have invited to sign the contract.—That's all, that simple.
We just make it a "fait accompli" and ask the Worldbank for approval."

"Lic. Nota, I want you to redact this in a proper way as we speak.

Ing. Sigul you take this afternoon's Lacsa flight to Miami, so avoiding Mr. Ahmed who travels on Pan Am.
You take the very next flight to Washington, call Petersen first thing in the morning and submit this proposal."

"Ing. Caldera I want you to telex JB, declaring the contract and allocation null and void. Their tampering with the bid has been discovered which automatically disqualifies them as bidder.
We reserve the right to demand indemnification."

Their meeting was concluded. Andy Quarry felt much better.

He had orchestered this "salida" the way he was used to do things.
If his gut feeling did not deceive him, his strategy would work.
It could not be in the Worldbank's interest to affront their country.
His proposal would everybody help to save its face.

He had not been given this job only for being Don Jepe's friend.
All the years he had well been capable to run ITE.
He had made a mistake but he was still able to correct it himself.

◆   ◆   ◆

Sigul had to rush to get the Lacsa afternoon flight. His secretary was able to get him reservations and a ticket all the way to Washington. He was scheduled to arrive there on an Eastern Airlines flight around 10 pm.
This visit to the Worldbank was different than to the ones he had done before.
The arrogant way Ahmed had declined his invitation was a way of saying that he did not want to associate with people who took bribes.
He had no idea what reaction his unannounced visit most likely even before Ahmed reported back might provoke.
He only could hope that the note he was supposed to deliver was received the way Quarry was anticipating.
What if Petersen and Ahmed made him the scapegoat for everything?
He always had been the link between ITE and Worldbank.
They might well confront and blame him that a tampered with bid had made it from recommendation, to allocation and contract signing to their desk asking for the bank's approval.

He was going into a lion's cave.

Caldera was smart. Although he would have received the main part of the "commission", he had managed to put him in front.

After a six hour flight not counting the two hour wait in Miami, it was around midnight when he checked into a hotel not far from the World bank in downtown Washington.

Shortly after 9 am the next day he called Petersen who had just entered the office. He was very surprised to learn that Sigul was just steps away and was asking for an urgent meeting.

"What is it in regard to Mr. Sigul?"

"I am supposed to deliver an official note and proposal in answer to your note delivered by Mr. Ahmed. This note and proposal should be considered before Mr. Ahmed makes his report."

"Give me some time to talk to Mr. Ahmed first. Why don't you stop by in an hour, say 10.30 am."

◆   ◆   ◆

About the same time Sigul was making his appointment with Petersen, Ernie entered his office in Schenectady. He was just coming back from his trip to Essen.

He quickly looked through his mail and checked the messages. Then he went to HH's office and reported about his trip to Germany.

HH was not too happy about their arrangements with Maldecara, but had to admit that working with his old foe, their chances in Venezuela would improve.

Chapter 6
Will Breaks rocks

Sigul had been many times at the Worldbank. He usually made this visit to either clarify technical questions or in some occasions to promote ITE's projects for Worldbank loans. He normally was glad to have this break from his daily routine work at his home office.

This time it was different.
When he was led into a small conference room and waited for Petersen and possibly Ahmed, he had an odd feeling. What when they declared this tender null and void or simply put them on a black list, denying any future financing.

They would literally slaughter him, his boss Quarry, the media and all the others who were desperate to get the San Antonio power plant.
They would demote him or simply kick him out of ITE.

And for the country: The worst would only come in about ten month, when the hydroelectric power stations ran dry, when there was no more power to run the slaughter houses. Cattle farming and meat export was next to coffee farming and Bananas Costa Rica's most important income source.
The hospitals without power, the entire country without power.

This time he was totally at the mercy of Ahmed and Petersen. If they only gave him a chance. He had to have the word first. He knew exactly how to avoid being put against the wall.

But if they would open their meeting and immediately blame ITE for all the wrong doings—then they did not have any choice but to declare this tender null and void.
All this went through his head when he was waiting.—And they let him wait.

Was this a good sign, did they also try to find a strategy how to avoid all these consequences or was this to soften him for worse things to come.

Then there was a knock at the door and Petersen followed by Ahmed entered the room.

"One can have real adventures, in your country," opened Petersen the meeting, "I had no idea that one can get lost that easily in your jungles.
Sorry to keep you waiting, but Mr. Ahmed told me very briefly about his odyssey in the rain forest.—
What is it, Mr. Sigul, that you could not discuss with Mr. Ahmed in San Jose and why this trip and meeting."

Sigul was obviously nervous and was anything but at ease. Nevertheless that was the opening he had hoped for.

"We were very concerned when we learned about Mr. Ahmed's excursion to the volcano Barva and the entire country was with great sorrow when he and his friend had simply disappeared. Our entire police force, as you know we have no military, was only after three days able to find them.
Many people lose their way in our "selvas" and are never seen again.
But it is much worse if something like this happens to our guests."
We are glad that everything came to a good end.

But the reason of Mr. Ahmed's visit was to audit the San Antonio tender.
The fact that we were being audited by the Worldbank, although known only by the people directly involved with this project, was as such very embarrassing for us. I personally felt hurt that Mr. Ahmed, due to these special circumstances had to avoid me—we were not even able to have a personal chat.
It was therefore for me a question of honor to find out if there was any wrongdoing during the evaluation or allocation of this tender.
Thanks to Mr. Ahmed's longer than planned trip into our rainforests, I should not say this, we had time to do our own investigation.
This is what we found out:

At tender opening the best offer by price, time of delivery and adherence to the technical as well as legal part was presented by the consortium lead by EG. They ranked first among all bidders.

At some point one of the bidders, JB, requested, based on updated technical specifications from their license holder General Electric, to modify their technical tender specifications.
Since Manis partner in the EG consortium and also MA (manufacturing associate) of GE, was asking for the same, we gave JB permission.

It did not make any sense for JB to make these modifications, since EG who at this point had the best bid, followed suit. JB would not have been able to improve its ranking against EG.
So there had to be a different reason to get hold of the tender documents.

Questioning all personnel in our department as well as security people and secretaries, we found out that JB abused our trust and did not only do the technical modifications permitted, but also replaced original and sealed pages of their bid and by doing this practically rewriting and improving their bid.

This led to their allocation.

Only yesterday a summary of all these facts was presented to Andy Quarry my boss, when Mr. Ahmed already had left our country.
The information was held back on purpose by the same engineers who are to blame for what happened.

We immediately informed JB, declared the allocation null and void and asked them to leave Costa Rica as soon as possible. Their representative Juliano Maldecara, who masterminded all this, was declared "persona non grata" and is forbidden to enter our country.

The EG bid was from the first moment and still is in every respect the most favorable bid.

We intend to officially allocate this tender to the EG consortium and invite them to sign a contract with us.'

"That the price sheets had been tampered with was immediately obvious to me when I reviewed the JB bid." answered Abdul Ahmed, the Worldbank's referent for Central America.
"I do not understand that it took you so long to find that out.

I can not deny that I have the impression and I had it when I did this audit that you all were very interested to do this business with JB."

"Well I think we have spent a lot of time for this in Worldbank terms relatively small project in Costa Rica." intervened Mr. Petersen, the Worldbank's director for Latin America.

"What I take from your verbal report Mr. Ahmed, you also place the EG consortium's bid on first place.

Why don't we leave it at this?

ITE should proceed as Mr. Sigul reported.

There is certainly a lot to blame ITE for.

But we want to be of help.

If everything is correctly handled from now on, and Mr. Sigul get me right, there remain many things which are not outspoken,—ITE can go ahead and allocate this tender to EG..

You have our blessing."

Sigul was relieved, he had what he needed. This was the only way out of this self inflicted dilemma. He had an introverted almost shy personality.

He had followed Caldera. Caldera had been contacted by Maldecara.

Caldera needed the money. He wanted to go into politics.

Sigul had been happy the way things were. He liked his job as head of the engineering team.

Thanks god, once this problem solved—he would never do anything like this again.

He had dinner at his hotel, went early to bed and took the first morning flight to return to San Jose.

Since there was a time difference of two hours, he was able to meet the same day with his boss and also with his engineers.

They agreed to immediately allocate the tender to the EG consortium and ask EG to enter as soon as possible in contract negotiations.

Directly after their meeting was finished, he called Mrs. Croman, the consortium's agent and gave her the news.

"We lost precious time; the power station has to generate electricity in less than 10 month. The contract has to be negotiated and signed not later than 2 weeks from now.
Please get hold of Messrs. Golden and Piper; they should take the next flight. We want to start negotiations on Monday."

Mrs. Croman called immediately Golden in Germany, waking him with the good news in the middle of the night.

Golden couldn't believe what she said, but agreed to take the next flight to San Jose.

Then she called Ernie.
"I have been waiting for this call; I knew that our strategy would work.
ITE had to give in sooner or later.
The problem is, I am now working on a different project and I never get permission to take this business up again.
I urge you to ask Mr. Sigul or Mr. Quarry to call my boss and to give him personally this terrific news.
If they ask him to send me, to do the contract, he might let me go."

That was too much for the old lady.
"If you people don't believe what I am telling you, that is your problem. We have done everything one can ask for.
I gave you the information and request as I received it from ITE, now the ball is in your court."
And she hung up.

Nevertheless first thing when Ernie entered the office, he met HH and gave him the news as he received it.

He probably caught HH on the wrong foot:
"Ernie don't you ever bother me again with this Costa Rica business. I saw your expense report. You spent more for taxi on your last trip than the entire company in one year. I am not interested in that business which was lost from the beginning.
What Jordan told me about this old lady, she is nuts—how can you believe such a nonsense."

That was it. Ernie also had his doubts. There had been too many ups and downs in this business.

He would do one last thing: call Lappa to verify the information given by their agent.

Nobody answered Lappa's telephone.

He could not reach Golden either.

Golden was already on his way to Central America.

◆   ◆   ◆

In the meantime in Costa Rica:

Both newspapers La Nacion and La Republica reported on their front pages about the power shortages and continuous black outs the country was presently facing. They reported that the hydro electric power station "Cachi" was almost dry.

And—that the thermal power station San Antonio which was supposed to solve these problems starting next dry season would be late, probably never built.

They reported that President Figueres and ITE's president Andy Quarry were involved in a corruption scandal and that Ahmed, the man who had been lost in the rainforest was now back in Washington, probably canceling the bank's agreement with Costa Rica.

The Scottish company who had signed the contract with ITE had been kicked out of the country.

Most likely somebody from the opposition party was behind this story.

The entire country was in uproar. Everybody was suffering from the power shortages and was hoping that this at least was the last dry season under these conditions.

The opposition Christian Democrats and the Communist Party called even for President Figueres' resignation. ITE's president urgently arranged for a press conference.

"It is true the allocation for JB was declared null and void. The tender will be allocated to an American/German consortium. This allocation has already been approved by the Worldbank. Contract negotiations will start Monday next week."

Sigul called Mrs. Croman to confirm that Ernie's and Jim's arrival before Monday.
When he heard that Piper probably would not come, since he needed permission from his boss to travel, he asked for Piper's phone number.
He called Piper in the office only to learn that Piper was not allowed anymore to touch this project.

Now Sigul was panicking. He had not thought that a bidder might refuse to take the business. What now.
He called HH, EG's president.
He explained in all details what had happened and almost begged him to let Ernie travel and do the contract negotiations.

Whatever HH had said before to Ernie—it was forgotten.
HH was impressed.
"I have been long in this business, never have I heard of anything like that:
-Involving 2 heads of state,
-losing.
-Formal allocation to competitor.—
-Involving the top guys from the Worldbank.
-Investigation,
-country in uproar,
-customer "begs" us to come and sign contract."

To Sigul he said:
"Excuse me Mr. Sigul, but there have been so many ups and downs in this business, as long as we do not have anything in writing, we are not going to touch this anymore.
Send me a telex, signed by your president, stating that this tender is allocated to our consortium and that you request the presence of Mr. Piper in order to start contract negotiations on Monday."

In less than an hour HH had the telex he asked for signed by ITE's president.

"Ernie I take everything back, I have learned something new, you surely impressed me.
You are free to travel, good luck."

Chapter 7
The Contract

What a difference.—
When Ernie last traveled this route, he was depressed and had just experienced one of his greatest disappointments ever.

This time he felt good, a winner.

He had fought on all fronts:
the client, the competitors, their agent; the Worldbank,
-and worst his own people, instead of backing him, they had caused him the worst time.

He had to fight for every bit of support:
From the client—all he found was the subordinate Lappa, who had fed him with some information.
Nota initially in his boat—turned against him.
He had to fight for every bit of support from their agent.
The two weird ladies who turned out to be more of a nuisance than help.
His ideas, his will had prevailed.
Oh, it felt so good.

All the moments of defeat: When the allocation went to his competitor, when the visit to the Worldbank did not show the expected results, when he had to take the blame from his boss
-it all was it worth for the joy and satisfaction he felt now.
Only somebody with the same kind of drive for success, to fight, to win at all cost, can understand how he felt.
And these moments were energizing.
He had been like a discharged battery—and now he was charging.

A famous man once said: "who does not want to fight—is not worth living."

Ernie's most difficult fight was the one against his own temptations: to give up, to simply have a good time and forget the business; to enjoy the beautiful country, the girls—oh Costa Rica had so much to offer.

As intensely as he fought as intensely he was now going to enjoy everything this trip to Costa Rica had to offer.

Late afternoon he arrived at El Coco, Ticaraguas international airport.
Jim was there to pick him up.
Jim and Ernie had become good friends.
Jim had gone through all the ups and downs like Ernie.
He was now fully enjoying the new situation.
All their adversaries Caldera, Sigul and Nota, had done everything imaginable to show that they were now willing to cooperate. They had invited Jim home, the week end they had him taken to their fincas.
Jim had access to their offices at all times. He never had to call ahead. They were foes turned into friends.
Jim's broad smile had become permanent.

On the way to the hotel he briefed Ernie about everything they had not been able to talk one the phone.

"I have a copy of the contract put into your room, so you can review it and make your own notes. They want start discussing the legal and commercial part tomorrow.
As far as the technical part is concerned, there are lots of queries regarding erection, assembly, civil part etc. I am waiting for Tomble to find local partners especially for his civil part. There was much time lost with JB. Now we have to make good for everything."

When they arrived at the hotel Europa, a great surprise was waiting for Ernie.
Olga, now a proud flight attendant had a day off and sat in the lobby. With a joyful cry she jumped into Ernie's arms to welcome him with a hot and deep kiss.

They registered and went up to their room. As a courtesy they were up-graded into the presidential suite.

Ernie and Olga had not seen for quite a while.

So many things had happened in the meantime.

They fell into each others arms and kissed now being without spectators. They hastily undressed and enjoyed making love which both had missed for a long time.

Early next morning they had breakfast together with Jim. Olga had a morning flight to New Orleans and had to leave soon. They kissed goodbye, this time knowing that it was only a short time they were separated.

Ernie was supposed to meet with Lic. Nota at 10 am. This gave him enough time to mark the legal and commercial contract part where ever he wanted changes. He made respective notes and then went together with Jim to the ITE offices.

When they entered the old building at parque Morales, the receptionist who always had greeted them friendly, this time stood up and said:
"I am so glad you are back, Don Ernesto, it is so much nicer to see you now every day than these jerks from JB."

When they entered Nota's office, the secretary even embraced him and offered him her cheek for a welcome kiss.
Nota stormed out of his office embraced Ernie and with a broad smile, welcomed him:
"Ernesto we have been waiting so impatiently for you. You can not imagine how glad we are to have you back."
He ordered coffee for all of them, but before the coffee arrived, the door opened and somewhat shy and a little embarrassed but nevertheless smiling all over his face, Caldera came in. He shook Ernie's hand and said:
"Senor Piper now you took your revanche showing us who needs whom. I do not blame you after all what happened. Let's work together. I promise I will cooperate."

"We were just on different sides, now we are in one boat," answered Ernie.

"We have the same goal: To get this contract done as soon as possible, so we can start building the power station.
I am glad we are finally together after we gave each other such a hard time."

"I have great respect for you Don Ernesto", answered Caldera, "amazing how you got what you wanted."

And again the door opened and Sigul entered together with Juarez Tejido ITE's general manager.

"Finally he is here. Your boss gave us a hard time. He could not believe we wanted to do business with him. He should be more confident and proud to have people like you, working for him.
Welcome and if there is anything I can help you with do not hesitate, come and see me."
This was Juajez Tejido's welcome. So far he was little involved in this project but as Gerneral Manager he was now playing an import part.

"Don Andy Quarry can not personally welcome you," said Sigul, "As you know he is in his late sixties and his health is not too good any more. Knowing everything will be now in good hands he took a few days off and went to his finca at the volcano Arenal. You Caldera and I will be working closely together to finalize this contract. If there is anything you do not agree with, see me, I am sure if there is a will there is also a way.
As you showed us, Senor Piper."

Ernie could not ask for more. That was an unexpected more than friendly welcome. What a difference, what a difference....

Then they left Nota's office. The coffee was still untouched and in the meantime, cold.

Nota and Ernesto took seat next to each other and together read the contract, page by page. Ernesto made his observations—Nota took notes. Time went by quickly.
Jim had gone back to the hotel to call the subcontractors and later to pick up Twomble at the airport. Twomble was the consortiums partner for the civil—and erection work.

Lic Tulio Cesar Nota, who was now just Don Tulio and Ernie, now being Ernesto, agreed that the latter would provide his own text for the commercial part of the contract.

So Ernesto took a taxi and went also back to the hotel.

He called their agent to say hello. and ask for a secretary.

Mrs. Croman was upset that he had not called earlier and was not willing to provide a secretary.

Ernie contacted Sandra, the hotel operator. Sandra had become a valuable good friend. She took notes of all calls—and there were many, she paged him and she gave him all kinds of tips and advice.

Sandra found him a secretarial service which fortunately was next door to the hotel Europa.

Ernie took all paperwork and simply went to meet his temporary secretary.

He started his dictation immediately and stopped only when it was almost too late to have dinner in one of the nearby restaurants.

Later he met with Jim and Twomble at the hotel bar. They had discussions till after mid night about payment terms, penalty clauses and price escalation clauses.

Early the next day Ernest resumed his dictation job which again lasted till the late evening. The rest of the evening went similar as the day before.

The following morning when his contract draft was finished and copied he took a cab to Nota's office.

Again they went through it page by page, sometimes they had to consult Caldera, agreed on changes and finally the legal and commercial part were ready, agreed upon between Lic. Tulio Nota, ITE' syndicus and head of ITE's legal department and Ernesto Piper for the EG—consortium.

They were the two responsible who would also officially sign for this part of the contract.

The technical part of the contract did not require any changes .—The tender documents were taken as is, to form that part of the contract.

Everything went much better and faster then expected. Nota had to prepare the final paperwork for the contract to be signed and set a date.

The date was set for the following week, July 18.

The date for the tender opening had been December 5th, the previous year.
More than 7 month had gone by. An extraordinary long time for such a business.
The time alone spoke for itself. What a struggle.
With a continuous period of more than 4 month at the Hotel Europa, Ernesto
was regarded as a permanent resident in Costa Rica and a stranger at home.

The 4 days till the signing of the contract was supposed to take place, went by
with countless meetings with all kinds of subcontractors. Prices and delivery
times were negotiated, local manufacturing plants were visited.

Every evening was booked with invitations to the homes of Nota, Caldera, Lappa
and the Croman ladies.
After these social obligations Ernie met usually with Olga. She picked him up at
the hotel and showed him all sort of romantic places. Mostly late at night they
returned to the hotel where they spend the rest of the night together. It was a very
intense and beautiful time.

Then came the famous day—the day they had been fighting for, waiting for, the
day they had dreamed of—the day of signing the contract.

It was a Wednesday. Jim and Ernie had breakfast at the hotel. They wore their
best suit, white shirt and tie. Given the hot and humid July weather without any
air conditioning, this was anything but pleasant.

They took Jim's rental car and went to the ITE offices where they were immediately led to the board room "sala de la junta".
Everything was solemnly decorated. The country's flag was at the head end of the
conference table. A TV crew was putting their cameras in the right position.
Microphones were placed at the head end of the table.

Caldera, Nota, Sigul and Juarez Tejido were already there. So were many other
people they never had met before. The two Croman ladies were there chatting
with Lic. Guzman who was not only the lawyer of ITE's board of directors but
also their lawyer.

There was a lot of handshaking; courtesies were exchanged the usual small talk.
Somebody from the TV crew came and asked Jim and Ernie for an interview
after the signing ceremony.

Two reporters one from La Nacion the other one from La Republica asked for the same.

The board room was brightly illuminated which caused an almost unbearable heat. The air was bad with many more people than the room was made for and the formal dressing did the rest.

Jim and Ernie took their coats off and went outside to get some fresh air.

The ceremony was set for 10 am; it was almost 11.30 am when Lic. Nota came and asked Ernesto and Jim in.

The moment they all had waited for so long was finally there.

The contract would be signed by Juarez Tejido, Sigul and Nota for ICE and by Jim and Ernie for the EG consortium.

Nota was supposed to read the entire contract (more than 40 pages). Ernie was placed between him and Juarez Tejido to carefully listen and when necessary make objections. Jim sat on the other side together with Ing. Sigul. He also was supposed to make objections when necessary.

And then Nota started and read with his loud and clear pastoral voice for more than an hour. Ernie was fighting sleep and so did Jim and many others.

At almost 1 pm it was over.

The contract was passed around and signed.

Every page had to be initialed.

Flashlights were blinking, the TV camera was buzzing.

They shook hands, flashlights were blinking again.

Ernie and Jim gave the interviews they had been asked for, very brief—everybody was hungry and tired. It had been a long ceremony.

The Croman ladies had a festive lunch at their home prepared.

All important ITE functionaries as well as Jim and Ernie were invited.

◆   ◆   ◆

Ernie's job was done.

The execution of the contract would be the job of one of his colleagues.

That was routine work. They had built many power stations all over the world.

There would be problems which somehow would be solved.

That was different with Jim. His job was only complete when the four gas turbine units generated electricity and a formal turn key hand over to ITE was done. He still had plenty worries whether delivery times could be met, the efficiency rates were as promised and what other at this point unforeseeable events might occur.

Both were on board of a plane to Miami. There they would change planes, Jim continuing to Germany and Ernie to New York.

Now the business they had so much fought for in their pocket, they felt a certain emptiness and nostalgia.
They had so much got used to the excitement to the intense way of living, the exotic tropical country, the beautiful girls simply to the adventurous way of living and doing business.

Both had been lost in their thoughts. Jim broke the silence:
"We are the most fortunate people I can think of.
Who in these times where everything is done by its rules will ever get a chance to set his own rules and prevail?
Who will ever live an exciting and gratifying life as we did the last eight months?
I am going to have great problems to return to the boring routine life.
I will miss your way of doing things, to always find a way out or a solution nobody dreams of and to lead an adventurous life as exciting as in the days of the great explorers."

"Cheer up old boy! We have made a perfect team. Let's continue working together; doing business the way we did will always be adventurous.
We have two more projects where we agreed to work together:
One in Venezuela and the other one in Colombia.—

I can already smell the adventure."

Fact

-hijacking of Lanica plane
-fight and liberation
-Maldecara story
-involvement of high ranking
-politicians
-public tender, bribing, contract

Fiction

-David Levy story
-Ahmed/Weller story

About the Author

Born at the German/French border multilingual, economist. Started writing non-fiction adventure stories from African Sahara and Sahel before selling multi million infrastructural projects in Africa and South America requiring access to top government officials. This made him an expert in this highly corruptive business. He is now writing his adventurous stories from his home in Florida from where he still communicates with all the places he once called home.

978-0-595-40679-1
0-595-40679-3

www.ingramcontent.com/pod-product-compliance
Lightning Source LLC
Chambersburg PA
CBHW030943180526
45163CB00002B/688